Natural Order and the Return of Independent City-States:

What Will Americans Do Next?

Edward R. Straka

June 17, 2025

I would like to thank Rebecca Price for her editorial assistance. Any flaws in my arguments remain mine alone.

Let them ask, then, whether it is quite fitting for good men to rejoice in extended empire. For the iniquity of those with whom just wars are carried on favors the growth of a kingdom, which would certainly have been small if the peace and justice of neighbors had not by any wrong provoked the carrying on of war against them; and human affairs being thus more happy, all kingdoms would have been small, rejoicing in neighborly concord; **and thus there would have been very many kingdoms of nations in the world, as there are very many houses of citizens in a city.**

Augustine
City of God Book IV: 15

On June 23rd, 2016 Britain voted against staying within the European Union.[1] Their reasons were many, beginning with cultural issues but equally economic, ethnic, and political. In spite of dire warnings by opponents both domestic and abroad of how Britain can't make it alone – in spite of ruling an overseas Empire for 300 years! – the votes came in and Britain is no longer subject to Brussels and their bankers and their unelected politicians. Perhaps even more interesting is the fact that London voted against leaving the EU and now many Brits want London to secede from Britain as they are viewed to be in opposition to the general will of the British people.[2]

---

[1]
http://www.nytimes.com/2016/06/25/world/europe/
britain-brexit-european-union-referendum.html
[2] http://www.mirror.co.uk/news/uk-news/londoners-
call-capital-break-away-8276156

Many now ask which other European countries, given their own economic and political problems as well as unwanted migrant problems, will follow as more and more Europeans grow tired of what they view as the EU leaders' unwanted controls.[3] Will it collapse? The head of the European Central Bank, Mario Draghi believes it might.[4]

And now – Donald Trump is the President of the United States for the second time! What will this mean long-term?[5] Perhaps the real issue is whether this movement could spread to some of the States within the U.S.A.[6] At first blush that seems

---

[3]
http://www.express.co.uk/news/world/683224/END-OF-THE-EU-Germany-France-Austria-Hungary-Finland-Netherlands-Europe-Brexit
[4]
https://www.armstrongeconomics.com/international-news/europes-current-economy/draghi-admits-eu-may-breakup-for-first-time/
[5]
https://www.lewrockwell.com/2017/01/no_author/support-calexit-jumps/

laughable, until one realizes that both the population size of some of the states related to other countries as well as their economic prowess compared to other independent nations abroad is very similar.

Is such a thing far-fetched given the growing frustration in America with Washington D.C. not to mention the ethnic, cultural and political differences? Even more important to consider – how would such a thing take place?[7]

This booklet acts as an inquiry into the subject of the return of the Independent City-States and will use philosophers from throughout history to suggest why this should be the case.

---

[6] https://www.lewrockwell.com/2012/11/thomas-dilorenzo/the-american-tradition-of-secession/

[7] https://mises.org/blog/first-uk-then-scotland-then-texas

Natural Order and the Return of Independent City-States:

What Will Americans Do Next?

Introduction

As had been noted in *America's Age of Empires*, the current structure of American society is definitively centralized compared to what it was in the past. Granted, compared to other centralized and authoritarian states – at whatever level – America is the most free. Nonetheless, our historic freedoms have long passed away and what governs America's political concerns today, both domestic and abroad, are both special interest and agenda based in orientation rather than that which is important to most people, most of the time in their everyday lives. This can be seen in the vehemence of the current presidential race and the violence occurring in our streets as accusations and demands are hurled back and forth with regard to what every American supposedly deserves.[8]

There is a tendency when things go bad in a civilization for the people to attempt to freeze any attempt at real change by clinging to the past in the name of "patriotism." But as was also discussed in *America's Age of Empires*, what form of patriotism? Being patriotic about and over what? Even more importantly, what if change – economic, political, and social - is a foregone conclusion and there is nothing that ultimately can be done to stop it?

In *America's Age of Empires*, I discussed the historiography of the late Carroll Quigley[9] and looked at civilization

---

8 http://www.acton.org/pub/religion-liberty/volume-26-number-2/what-our-constitution

in general, and America's development in specific as a three step trajectory of the following three categories:

Community

Nation

Empire

Likewise, I dealt with the four-point process wherein all countries/nations proceed on their way to the Empire category or back down to the national level alone, or even the total collapse of that civilization:

Core

Expansion

Crisis

Reset/ or Collapse

---

9 Carroll Quigley, *Tragedy and Hope: A History of the World in Our Times*, (New York, NY: The MacMillian Company 1966). Carroll Quigley, *The Evolution of Civilizations,* (Indianapolis, IN: Liberty Fund, 1979).

Quigley's perspective, and mine, is that there is a normal flow of civilization before collapse. A community – however great or small – forms around a leader that stakes out a territory and essentially sets up a society based upon certain philosophical principles (economic, legal, religious) that act as a solidifying agent to the society. These "principles" become the social norms or Core Values that are foundational to the societies survival as a community.

Equally of note, it is when the core values are strongest that you will have a time of great expansion of that community into a town or even, over time, a city. Eventually that city begins to influence the surrounding area (here in the States, a county or parish). From there it spreads out further to become a province or state. From there it becomes, unless a major crisis destroys it – a civilization.

This age of expansion is marked by four kinds of expansion:

Population

Geographic Area

Production

Knowledge

These four concepts drive the expansion from the core area to the semi-peripheral (neighboring area) to the outward areas (total peripheral).

My point was and remains that once a civilization has moved on to the "total peripheral" area it has become an empire with little resemblance to that which provided the internal dynamism to build a civilization in the first place. Equally, once a civilization has become an empire, its populace so diverse, and social norms and customs so diffuse in the name of "tolerance," it no longer resembles the original community of values that originally built it in the first place. It has become something else with a limited lifespan that not only ends up destroying itself as do all large-scale politico-economic systems, but the communities within become alienated from one another as they are driven by new values in general, and the State in specific regarding both domestic and international programs.

As noted in *America's Age of Empires*, a community is, in terms of natural progression, the end result of individuals who gather together in a specific geographic area. They marry people and then have children who likewise marry and thus form clans which band together to form tribes or communities who set down roots which they then proceed to develop and take dominion over territory and form towns as the outgrowth of the founding community.

Yet these small communities, living organisms of human relationships that must be built and maintained through human interaction, would in time grow and expand to well beyond their original size. With this expansion came a greater social influence, as the cultural patterns of these communities took root psychologically and relationally amongst the people in the area, as did the desire to stay and solidify into something bigger than themselves: the City.

Historically, the city represented a common life amongst a group of people who had decided to continue to live together in a specific location. Their reasons for living together were many: economic benefits via the division of labor, geographic conveniences, safety in numbers, camaraderie, mutual aid and last but certainly not least, a similar world and life view.

Granted, people can live anywhere they want and in any type of structure that they please. Yet it should cause concern that what was once taken for granted regarding the relationships of families, friends and neighbors that spanned generations has now been replaced by a highly mobile, essentially rootless culture that pursues its quest for autonomy and self-gratification which puts at risk the more vulnerable members of society. This is a dangerous thing because it strikes at both a historical reality, as well as a theological one that has maintained community life, and the effects of community life, for thousands of years throughout the world.[10]

In terms of society, communities – similar to marriages – functioned best when they served to establish family and social life on a sound economic basis, created kinship, and provided for intergenerational

---

[10] See: *Suburban Sprawl and New Urbanism* (vol.45) along with *Place, Community and Memory* (vol.3) of Mars Hill Audio, P.O. Box 7826, Charlottesville, Virginia 22906-7826.

bonding, intergenerational ties, intergenerational continuities that grounded communities on a solid foundation. All of this served to prevent the rise of rootless people wandering from here to there, thus unable to make a stand and firmly establish a community with its own culture; a scenario that has always weakened a society.[11]

In other words, cities in Europe and in early America were once designed for the purpose of community life being an opportunity to live out the Christian virtues (I Cor.13) as well as for mutual support and

---

[11] "Families were uprooted from the land, left the ancestral cemeteries and church, began to lose their faith as they turned to the new gods of money, school, and jobs, turned from the Bible to the government, from eternity to careers. This is a very old sequence, and every civilization has undergone this change..." Otto Scott, "The Family & History," Tape #7, from the Sociology Course class of Whitefield College (World View Productions: Lakeland, Florida).

defense (or, Islamic virtues if Muslim, or Jewish virtues if Hebrew, and so on). I am referring to the beliefs, values, etc. of societal groups and of the processes governing social phenomena – in other words, the *ideas* behind what we see in our culture around us, and how those ideas generate the lifestyles visible to everyone.

Given that modern America cannot even decide which bathroom to use, not to mention what is an appropriate, Constitutionally – based foreign policy as well as "who owes who" what or anything in terms of past transgressions of one ethnic group against another – it seems obvious that the "American Experiment" is over. Indeed, if we talk about "our country" – what does that even mean? Who is it that decides what the word "our" means? We certainly will receive no help from our public school system that turns out millions of functionally illiterate graduates a year not to mention indoctrinates these same graduates with every anti-traditional American philosophy under the sun.

And then there is the media and Hollywood…

It is the social norms, or ideas that grew out of such an arrangement of people, places and things that would establish what the late historian and writer Carroll Quigley in his book *Tragedy and Hope* would call Core Values.[12]

Core Values are the psycho-spiritual beliefs, generally religious, and cultural norms, moral and social, that people arranged their community around. In many respects one could equally call this a form of Patriotism wherein one has a devotion to one's country or city that goes deeper than the surface level political beliefs and preferences and rather has a spiritual-

---

[12] Carroll Quigley, *Tragedy and Hope: A History of the World in Our Times*, (New York, NY: The Macmillian Company 1966), p. 4.

psychological component also, as Ernest Renan wrote over a hundred years ago:

A nation is a soul, a spiritual principle. Two things, which, it is true to say, only unite them, make up this soul, this spiritual principle. The one is in the past, the other is in the present. One is the common possession of the rich legacy of the past; the other is agreement in the present, the desire to live together, the will to continue to value the heritage received undivided...Therefore, a nation is a great unity, made up of the feeling of sacrifices one has made and of those that one would make again. A nation presupposes the past; however, it continues in the present because of a tangible fact: agreement, the clearly expressed desire to continue communal life.[13]

---

[13] Ernest Renan, "Discours et conferences. Qu'est-ce qu' ne nation?, Oeuvres", Tome I, p. 903f.

In other words, to *truly* have a unified people there needs to be a similar history that everyone could point to as a specific version of the past that they all share and take pride in. Equally important, and in some ways even more important, is the desire for a unified present with the hope of a shared future based upon both a plan for the future as well as a similar world and life view that everyone agrees to live in accordance with.

This "shared past" and "shared future" are inescapable aspects of town and/or city life and that "social bond" which is necessary if they are to continue beyond one generation as a manifestation of community in the true sense. For it is inescapably *the basis of the union* – some form of religious faith and love as well as community fellowship rather than the State,

---

Translation by Jean-Marc Berthoud, as quoted in: Calvinism Today, Vol. IV, No. 1, (January 1994): 3.

geographic location or force – that will determine the communion.[14] A decentralized union that arises out of such an arrangement of people, places and things can be deemed a Natural Order as opposed to the current "United States" union that is unified artificially thus, and similar to both Alexander the Great's Empire and the Roman Empire, fragmenting fast. This fragmentation should be of no surprise as the historical incidents noted above clearly show given that even the philosophers of old questioned the wisdom of centralization as opposed to the principle of decentralization found in the book of Micah (4:1-5) and the writings of various philsophers[15] throughout history.[16]

---

[14] http://www.nationalreview.com/article/435706/sebastian-junger-tribe-book

[15] Thomas Aquinas, prophetically anticipating America's own historic governing system, wanted a fairly decentralized construct in that he wanted both verticle and horizontal political participation with a king, aristocracy and the citizens. *ST*, I-II, 105.1.

The above noted "philosophers" believed there was a danger in allowing a city to grow too big due to the difficulty of not only managing it, but equally the tendency of rulers to grasp for more power. From there, the desire to project this power on neighboring cities or countries becomes problematic also.[17] Ultimately, the only way a social contract could be realized would be in a decentralized social structure rather than the continent sized suprastructure we currently live within.

This essay will attempt, in brief fashion, to set forth the principles of a decentralized structure of society which will allow a

---

[16] Aristotle, *Politics* 7:4; Plato, *Republic* 4:423a-c; *Laws* 737-740. With Aristotle, the concept was that everyone knew one another within the city thus there was a built-in check on anonymity amongst politicians/law-makers. Plato's desire is that the various social, economic and political functions can be carried out smoothly in times of peace or war not to mention appropriate land distribution amongst the populace.

[17] Augustine, *City of God,* Trans. Henry Bettenson, (London, England: Penguin Books, 1972; 1984), IV.xv.

natural order of relationships, communities and freedom to develop that will allow men and women to live freely and reach their potential as human beings rather than live as drones for the State.[18]

There will are five sections which set forth the principles introduced above:

1. The changing cultural landscape of modern America

2. An explanation of "Natural Order" in context of leadership

3. An explanation of Free States, City States & Charter Colonies

4. Why decentralization works best

5. Social Contracts/Covenants for living together

This essay will not discuss why the fragmentation of the current American Union and social order will ultimately reach critical, confrontation-wise, and

---

[18] https://www.lewrockwell.com/2016/06/ron-paul/fascism/

eventually decentralize[19] as that was already noted in *America's Age of Empires: the Loss of the Past.*

---

[19] http://dailycaller.com/2017/06/23/is-america-really-coming-apart-as-charles-murray-suggests/

Why Cultural Diffusion Always Leads to Cultural Collapse

Before attempting to address the above statement – perhaps the first question is: what exactly is culture?

According to the *American Heritage Dictionary*, "culture" is: 1. The totality of socially transmitted behavior patterns, arts, beliefs, institutions, and all other products of human work and thought characteristic of a community or a population. 2. A style of social and artistic expression peculiar to a society or class. 3. Intellectual and artistic activity, and the works produced by it. 4. The act of developing the social, moral, and intellectual faculties through education. 5. A high degree of taste and refinement formed by aesthetic and intellectual training (more was included in the definition regarding possible usage).[20]

That is one "dictionary definition" of culture, and one that speaks to most areas of a person's life, or sociology. But to the average person, culture is fine art, Greco-Roman buildings filled with old paintings and Steinway pianos, and glamorous people wearing the latest fashion sitting in a cappuccino bar, sipping wine or coffee, and speaking French, Mozart playing softly in the background.

Dr. Mary Ann Froechlich concurs:

---

[20] *American Heritage Dictionary, Second College Edition,* (Houghton Mifflin Co.: Boston, 1982,85), p.348.

In a wealthy, sophisticated society, a knowledge of the arts can be the sign of a cultured individual, contributing to one's image of power and success. The corporate executive who has built a billion-dollar company enjoys attending the symphony, playing Beethoven on his Steinway piano, and collecting fine artwork in the same way he enjoys nouvelle cuisine, good wine, traveling abroad, and having his library filled with classics. The arts are an indication of status.[21]

Yet the fact remains – "culture" is something more complex than so-called upper class culture and can have an affect, both positive and negative, on the society in

---

[21] Mary Ann Froehlich, *Music Education in the Christian Home,* (Wolgemuth-Hyatt Publishing: Brentwood, TN., 1990), p.8.

which a specific people group's culture begins to take hold.

We will begin our consideration of the "culture question" by examining culture from the perspective of *race* since that appears to be the most common denominator among the current socio-political controversy in America today, according to the 2016 presidential race talking points. My position will be that "race" is a faulty barometer for cultural superiority or inferiority.

Race and Culture

Is the cultural difference a matter of race? Some would say "yes" without hesitation. Indeed, many would attribute the problems America has, which were mentioned briefly above in the previous section, to the influx of peoples from other countries. Is this an accurate assertion? How often does each of us pause to consider what makes individuals or societies tick, what makes them so varied? Many of us follow current affairs on television or in a daily newspaper, but how far do we consider the concepts, beliefs, and attitudes that underlie and give shape to the actions, and even the decor of daily life in a society? Is the issue racial or something else?

Growing up in the Chicago-land area (Westside) in a predominantly white area, I was familiar with racial prejudice, and the usual off-color racial slurs. These words are nouns but were used more in an adjective sense to describe people who were of a different race, thus culture. As is the practice of the typical bigot, people tossed these labels about without even thinking about what they meant, and whether the derogatory label/ comment was even warranted. Reflecting back on it, the only reason why these labels were used was because the people being labeled were different. As to what the difference was, and whether it was good or bad or even true, that was never mentioned, much less discussed.[22]

But what really is culture, and is it racially determined?

Thomas Sowell, a senior fellow at the Hoover Institution at Stanford University, gives us his definition of culture below:

> Culture, as the term is used here, will not be confined to what one scholar on ethnicity has called "real culture," such as "music and art."

---

[22] "This attitude is known as *ethnocentrism*. It manifests itself in the form of racial prejudice, nationalistic fanaticism, religious intolerance, and various other social phenomena that keeps the peoples of the world from respecting and enjoying one another." *The Study of Sociology,* (Guilford, CT: Dushkin Publishing Group, Inc., 1974), p. 74. The writer raises a valid point about aspects of "ethnocentrism." However, the *primary* cause of that dislike between the races is SIN. This is ignored, of course, in the name of *cultural relativism.*

On the contrary, the focus here will be primarily on those aspects of culture which provide the material requirements for life itself – the specific skills, general work habits, saving propensities, and attitudes toward education and entrepreneurship – in short, what economists call "human capital." That is not because of a "glorification of the practical," conceived of as an antithesis to higher culture, but because the material resources from which physical survival itself must come are also requirements for music, art, literature, philosophy, and other forms of higher culture, rather than to meeting survival needs. Moreover, in comparing groups and societies, matters of subjective taste and habitual conditioning are so intimately involved in evaluations of music and art that it is far more problematical to speak of one group or society as being more advanced or more effective in these realms than to say that one group or society is more advanced in industrial skills or medical care.[23]

Sowell has pointed to the heart of the matter by suggesting that "Culture...not be confined to what one scholar on ethnicity has called "real culture," such as "music and art." But rather "on those aspects of culture which provide the material requirements for life itself – the specific skills, general work habits, saving propensities, and attitudes toward education and entrepreneurship – in short, what economists call "human capital." In other words, although "the arts are an indication

---

[23] Thomas Sowell, *Race and Culture: A World View,* (New York, NY: Basic Books, 1994), p.xii.

of status" as Dr. Froehlich stated earlier,[24] the enjoyment of these "arts" is one thing, the ability to produce them, along with maintaining their status as "higher culture" in the minds of society is quite another matter. This is particularly so if the issues of "human capital" are not recognized as a necessary foundation to a society's overall stability. A person may enjoy Mozart and Picasso, but if they cannot hold onto a job, or relate to other people in a polite manner, or solve a multitude of other problems on a regular basis that deal with everyday ordinary life, their "culture" will reflect these sociological patterns.

How this planes out will make many uncomfortable, particularly those tenured at liberal, leftist university campuses. As Sowell states:

---

[24] *Music Education in the Christian Home,* p.8.

It may sound noble to say that cultures are merely different, not better or worse in any way, and that it is all a matter of perceptions and preferences. But this argument contradicts itself by saying that one way of looking at cultural differences is *better* – the way of cultural relativism preferred by a fringe of contemporary intellectuals, rather than the way preferred by the vast majority of other human beings around the world and down through the centuries. These cultural differences do not matter only if cause and effect do not matter.[25]

---

[25] Thomas Sowell, *Migrations and Cultures,* (New York, NY: Basic Books, 1996), p. 381. Sowell's opinion is to the point! Why do "third world nations" (in *politically correct* jargon known as "LDNs" – less developed nations) – flock to the West (Europe, Britain, and the U.S.) if cultural differences do not matter?

In other words, many cultures are different, and indeed better, because they are not only different, but superior in the way they are able to solve their problems at every level of their sociology, while planning for the future with regard to health, education, law, and economics, not to mention the general well-being of the country. The more complicated the culture, the more complex the sociology (and therefore the people) will be.

All study of *sociology* will also point us to anthropology because it is man – *anthros* – who makes up society. And it is a society, and the people in it who produce a sociology and culture with something more foundational than art, music, and nightclubs. The Webster's New World Dictionary defines *sociology* as follows: "1. the science of human society and of social relations, organization, and change; specif., the study of the beliefs, values, etc. of societal groups and of the processes governing social phenomena..."[26]

Thus, we can say that "sociology" is part and parcel of who and what people are in the context of their daily lives. What people do in "the context of their daily lives" is what forms their personal culture that extends into, and leaves an impact upon their families, their workplace – assuming they work – and their community life, for better or worse. In other words, a person's daily habits are a reflection of their Core Values which will either work to develop and push a civilization above and beyond what it was before – or toward it's fragmentation.

In either case, cultural patterns determine the future of a community and its ability to hold itself together based upon previous cultural patterns. It is these "cultural patterns" that the citizens of the

---

[26] Webster's New World Dictionary, second edition, (New York, NY: Simon & Schuster, 1982), p. 1352.

community are patriotic about maintaining and thus desire to defend that precipitates the most conflict in our politically correct world.

On The Move

Upon considering the above, one is forced to consider the implications of the migrations of people, and their cultures, to new lands. The current migrant debacle in Europe is case in point: a tremendous number of illegal immigrants from Africa and the Middle East have essentially flooded the European landscape. Some countries, due to the obsession of the so-called leaders with multiculturalism, have opened their doors in the name of "humanity" and allowed any and all within their borders. Other countries have resisted. In either case – what will be the cultural result of such massive demographical shifts in the relationship between people, places and things in Europe? Do people really think that all will be the same in 50 years as one culture of totally different folkways impregnates another older, more traditional culture?

Even here in America, with the Southwestern states of America having a Latino population comprising anywhere from 1/3 to 3/4 of the total *known* (read: known by census) population,[27] and that being fairly *un*assimilated[28] with regard to

---

[27] Source: Population Estimates Program, Population Division, U.S. Bureau of Census, Washington, DC 20233; according to research done by the U.S. Census Bureau, Hispanics make up approximately 32% of the population of the Southwest as of 1990 (not including Texas) with New Mexico topping the list at 75%. Internet Release date: September 4, 1998: see http://www.census.gov/population/estimates/state/rank/sorh97.txt (Texas, in the 2000 census report, has population statistics that show a 54% increase compared to that shown in the 1990 census; see USA TODAY, Tuesday, March 13, 2001, p. 5A).

[28] See Otto Scott's newsletter *Compass*, both the January 1, 1997, vol.7, Issue 77, & July 1, 1998, vol.8, Issue 95, p.10-12; Uncommon Media, P.O. Box 69006, Seattle, WA 98168-1006. See also, Sol Sanders, *Mexico: Chaos on Our Doorstep*, (Ladham, MD: Madison Books, 1986).

language, culture, goals, and "allegiance to the country," it appears somewhat sophomoric to insist that these people are anything like that of the citizens of the eastern seaboard states, or the old "Confederate states" or the Midwest, or New York, New York. I am speaking of people who are citizens, or possibly would like to be but for reasons quite different than what brought my ancestors here long ago. Granted, this is nowhere near as critical as what Europeans currently face and yet, to suggest that there has not and will not be cultural change ignores all of history.

The 2010 Census showed both the continued, yet slipping population status of the descendants of the historic European settlers as well as the continued growth of the Hispanic and Asiatic American population:

The examination of racial and ethnic group distributions nationally shows that while the non-Hispanic white alone population is still numerically and proportionally the largest major race and ethnic group in the United States, it is also growing at the slowest rate. Conversely, the Hispanic and Asian populations have grown considerably, in part because of relatively higher levels of immigration.[29]

All of these people, both legal and illegal immigrants have their own reasons for being in America, and their own visions of what America is and should be. Many others come to America from countries (Africa, the Caribbean, China, India, the Middle East, Philippines, and so on) with

---

[29] https://www.census.gov/2010census/news/releases/operations/cb11-cn125.html

specific sociological concepts that are either "facilitators of, or obstacles to, progress."[30] Will these people change their sociology? Or will they change the sociology of the American people among whom they now live, although remaining separate in thought *and practice*?

Samuel Francis, a nationally syndicated columnist and editor, in his essay "Nation Within Nations" makes some rather alarming observations on the changes that are occurring in America due to the changing population:

> By the end of 1998, it was no longer possible for any informed and honest person to claim that the massive immigration experienced by the United States since the

---

[30] Lawrence Harrison, "Why Culture Matters," *Culture Matters: How Values Shape Human Progress,* a symposium edited by Lawrence E. Harrison and Samuel P. Huntington, (New York, NY: Basic Books, 2000), p. *xxi.*

1970's was not significantly altering the culture, economy, and politics of the nation. Last summer, the *Washington Post,* long a zealous opponent of immigration restriction, published a series of articles that effectively conceded the point: "Lives Transplanted, a Region Transformed. Steady Immigration Changes Face of the Region; Schools Add Up Immigrant Costs,' one headline informed its readers. The series, as well as other accumulating facts about immigrants not included in it, was not simply a confirmation of what supporters of immigration control have always suspected, indeed knew – that it is not humanely possible for millions of people from one culture to transplant themselves into another culture without

exerting some deleterious effect –
but actually pointed to an even more
important truth: Mass immigration
is not merely destroying one nation
but also is giving birth to a new one,
and the new nation will not be a
place where most Americans would
feel comfortable or even be
welcome.[31]

Is the above concern about race? And is
the matter of "race" and "racial problems"
an issue of skin color and geographic origin
as is commonly believed by both left-wing
and right-wing citizens, or the politicization
of the many races for the benefit of the few
involved in politics who seek votes to
acquire power?

Are there *preferred races,* for lack of a
better phrase, that we would rather live in

---

[31] Samuel Francis, "Nation Within Nations," an
essay from the January 1999 issue of *The Religion
& Society Report,* The Rockford Institute, Rockford,
IL.

community with? If so, who are they and why are they preferable? This is something to consider with regard to the future in the USA and how Americans view their "Socratic problem."[32] A quick look at Europe and the migration crisis of the past year as massive amounts of Middle Easterners force their way into Europe and bringing their own cultural patterns and practices with them shows the reality of shifting populations being able to destroy a historic culture all the while building a new one.[33]

This brings up the issue of *demographics;* a word derived from *demography* which means "the statistical science dealing with the distribution,

---

[32] The "Socratic Problem" simply stated is, "How can the individual be granted maximum freedom, yet be controlled by the rule of law for the good of society?" Kelley, M. *On Stone or Sand: the Ethics of Christianity, Capitalism, & Socialism*, (Carson, ND: Pleroma Press. 1993), p. 190.

[33] http://www.breitbart.com/london/2016/04/08/swiss-magazine-europe-abolishing-mass-immigration/

density, vital statistics, etc. of populations."[34] One can add to that definition the flow of money, intellectual capital, and work ethic along with tools and weaponry across borders; and the ability of certain peoples to hang on, long-term, to all of them.

Demographics is an area of study that must be considered carefully due to the complexity of people's lives, and how their personal beliefs and habits which they brought with them affect their heirs for generations to come. Indeed, a particular groups lifestyles are the manifestations of habits passed down generationally, as Sowell discusses in *Race and Culture,* from "environments that existed on the other side of an ocean, in the lives of ancestors long forgotten, yet transmitted over the generations,"[35] that show up in their daily

---

[34] Webster's New World Dictionary, second edition, (New York, NY: Simon & Schuster, 1982), p. 375.

lives. Will this situation have an adverse

---

³⁵ *Race and Culture,* p.x; Sowell writes using a philosophy that *contradicts* the prevailing social sciences which rely so heavily on environmental determinism as he explains here: "While we can all agree on the influences of "environment" in some very general sense, there is a vast difference between (1) regarding groups as being shaped by immediate circumstances, including the people and institutions around them, and (2) regarding groups as having their own internal cultural patterns, antedating the environment in which they currently find themselves, and transcending the beliefs, biases, and decisions of others. The vast migrations of peoples over the centuries have left many racial and cultural groups in settings radically different from the settings in which their own cultures evolved, facing challenges and opportunities undreamed of by their ancestors. Group cultural patterns may indeed be products of environments - but often of environments that existed on the other side of an ocean, in the lives of ancestors long forgotten, yet transmitted over the generations as distilled values, preferences, skills, and habits. The outward veneer of a new society – its language, dress, and customs – may mask these underlying differences in culture values, which are nevertheless revealed when the hard choices of life have to be made, and sacrifices endured, to achieve competing goals. Where an analysis is confined to one society – racial and ethnic groups in the United States, for example – it can be difficult to establish which patterns are the result of the way particular groups were treated in American society and which are the results of their own internal cultural patterns. But where the analysis is international in scope, then the group patterns which recur in country after country can more readily be distinguished from historical differences in the group's experience from one country to another."

affect on so-called "white America"? If so, in what way?[36] And is it the races that will affect the culture of "white America" or the *ideas* that the race in question live within that people of all color need to be concerned with? In other words, is it not their "sociology" as discussed above in the previous section, that will affect the *cultural norm* of America rather than their race?

Cultural Safety in Race or Worldview?

Perhaps even more to the point are the questions: *what exactly is white American*

---

[36] The concern, of course, is what will happen to American society, rather than the long gone "white America." As to the immigrants, depending upon where they come from, there indeed can be problems with how well they assimilate into our society, and the law system that upholds it. See: Seymour Martin Lipset & Gabriel Salman Lenz, "Corruption, Culture, and Markets," *Culture Matters: How Values Shape Human Progress.* Authors point out that "Countries dominated by a Protestant ethos are less corrupt than others." Page 120 – 122. Thus, by implication, those from non-Protestant nations will bring their corruption with them.

culture? Is being "white" the criteria for so-called "cultural safety" of the so-called "status quo culture" of middle-class America as the people I grew up with prejudicially believed?[37] Dr. Gary North does *not* think so as he focuses on the aspect of worldview and how "white America" changed decades ago:

> Culture, the product of cooperative human action, is vital to the tasks of domestication. Men are expected by God to set down roots, build for the future, establish permanent institutions, and increase in wisdom. From the beginning, men formed

---

[37] Interestingly enough, many in foreign countries, including European countries like France are as fearful of the destruction of their cultural identity by "gobalization" as Americans are via immigration. Indeed, many point the finger at America with regard to whose culture it is that they do *not* want. See: Mario Vargas Llosa, "The Culture of Liberty" in *Foreign Policy,* (Carnegie Endowment for International Peace: Washington, DC, Jan./Feb. 2001), p. 66-67.

communities. Cain built a city (Gen.4:17). Civilized men have always feared the life of nomadism. Cain pleaded with God that the life of a vagabond was more than he could bear as a punishment, and God graciously reversed this condemnation (Gen.4:12-15). It was too great a curse.

The advent of nomadism, especially the individualistic form, is a sign of social devolution. Chronologically, nomadism came later than civilization in human history, contrary to the religion of evolutionism. Nomadic tribes are often fierce warriors, but they leave few records of their own and no culture. The Huns, for example, left almost no trace of their years of conquest. The major history of the

Huns written in the twentieth century was a lifetime research project which was never fully completed by its author.[38] He had to master many languages in order to reassemble the story of the Huns, since there were only fragments available, in many geographical regions, written by victims and enemies of the Huns. Victorious on horseback, they were eventually swallowed up by the cultures they conquered leaving no literature of their own to testify to their importance.

The wandering tribe which operates in terms of the stripped earth policy (the North American plains Indians, for example) or theft (the gypsies) is

---

[38] Otto Manchen-Helfen, *The World of the Huns,* edited by Max Wright (Berkley: University of California Press, 1973).

clearly rebellious. Like the years of wandering in the wilderness by the Israelites, nomadism is a curse of God. Men who try to escape from the ethical burdens of laboring under the terms of the dominion covenant are often tempted to escape into this form of cultural rebellion. Hitchhiking in the United States has always been the practice of the poor, the hobos, the criminals, and the rootless young.[39] Police departments and other crime-fighting organizations have long warned drivers not to pick up hitchhikers, since there are so many criminals or disturbed, dangerous people among their ranks. It was no coincidence that in the years of the counter-culture, 1965-72, there

---

[39] See the "classic" document of the so-called "beat generation," Jack Kerouac's *On the Road* (New York: Viking, [1957] 1974).

were millions of teenaged youths on the roads of the Western nations, all looking for a free automobile ride to nowhere in particular. The nomad's life is a life of few responsibilities, which is why nomadism increased so rapidly when the counter-culture appeared.[40]

As the above quotation shows us, cultural deformation is more a "lifestyle" than a racial issue. Perhaps even more to the point, one could say it is a *mindset*. Indeed, and with the advent of high technology, and international business, it has become increasingly difficult to determine *whose culture is who*, as Ohmae illustrates for us below:

---

[40] Gary North, *The Dominion Covenant: Genesis* (Tyler Texas: Institute for Christian Economics, 1982/87) p.134 - 5.

But sooner than most people think, our belief in the "nationality" of most corporations will seem quaint. It is already out of date. Is IBM Japan an American or a Japanese company? Its work force of 20,000 is Japanese, but its equity holders are American. Even so, over the past decade IBM Japan has provided, on average, three times more tax revenue to the Japanese government than has Fujitsu. What is its nationality? Or what about Honda's operation in Ohio? Or Texas Instruments' memory-chip activities in Japan? Are they "American" products? If so, what about the cellular phones sold in Tokyo that contain components made in the United States by American workers who are employed by the U.S. division of a

Japanese company? Sony has facilities in Dotham, Alabama, from which it sends audiotapes and videotapes to Europe. What is the nationality of these products or of the operation that makes them? These are no longer anomalous situations. They have become commonplace, and they will become even more so. As Harvard professor Robert Reich has noted, "The very idea of 'American' firms is becoming obsolete. Lee Iacocca warns of the Japanese invasion of America, but American-made parts now constitute a smaller portion of the top models of the Big Three than they do of Honda's top-of-the-line cars."[41] Most companies in the Triad [referring to America, Europe, and Asia] are still financed by local

---

[41] "Members Only," *The New Republic,* June 26, 1989.

debt and equity and serve local markets with locally made goods produced by local workers. For them, nationality still has meaning. But for a growing population of firms that serve global markets or face global competition, nationality will disappear.[42]

As the quote above shows us, the determination of *cultural products* has also become very complex. Obviously, it was the Western world that developed the automobile, and the computer. Yet, it is the Japanese who have taken both products to the next levels of development, not the west![43] So obviously, when one looks from a historical perspective on both America's past dominance in the automobile industry,

---

[42] Kenichi Ohmae, *The Borderless World,* (New York, NY: Harper Business, 1990), p.10.

[43] Microsoft is not ignored here, however, there is computer technology beyond them that continues to develop.

along with high technology, and Japan's former international position in the market place compared to now, one is forced to reconsider if race really is the issue regarding certain aspects of cultural superiority, particularly in the economic realm. Many, of course, would say that it is due to the spread of technology, and although there is some merit to this argument, the basic premise is faulty.[44]

Perhaps even a better argument against the typical collegiate "oppressed masses have no access to technology" diatribe

---

[44] Even in a technological age, the diffusion of technology as such is not as important as the cultural receptivity of different nations, peoples, and cultures to that technology – their ability to take the technology, make it their own, modify it to suit their own purposes and circumstances, and develop it further on their own. Some nations and peoples have done this to a far greater extent than others, many of the latter being content to consume the products of more advanced technology, or perhaps to imitate the machinery that produced these products, following in the wake of others who continue to advance the technological frontier. See: *Race and Culture: A World View,* p.7.

against economically successful, thus culturally superior nations is as follows:

> Technology is of course not the sole determinant even of economic progress. Differences in work habits, savings propensities, organizational skills, personal hygiene, attitudes, and self-discipline all influence end results, both economic and social. Differences in all these respects influence economic and social outcomes among different groups within a given country, as well as among the nations of the world. These differences, however, are not static. Cultures spread, whether by assimilation of technology, the migrations of peoples, or the imposition of foreign cultures through conquest.

It would be enormously valuable to understand just why and how some cultures have seized the initiative at various periods of history and have led the technological, scientific, or medical advancement of the human race. Unfortunately, at the current stage of "social science," it is a struggle merely to establish that some cultures are in fact more productive in various ways than others, whether we are comparing the cultures of different nations or civilizations or the varying cultural achievements of different racial and ethnic groups within a given society. Yet differences have been the rule, rather than the exception, in countries around the world, though the magnitudes of these differences, and the reactions to them, have varied widely.[45]

In other words, we are back to the issue of *sociology* once again. *Sociology* as: "1. the science of human society and of social relations, organization, and change; specif., the study of the beliefs, values, etc. of societal groups and of the processes governing social phenomena..."[46] Given the disparity of cultural norms in the United States presently, and all the different perspectives as to both what America is as well as what it should be – I believe it is a given that we are no longer unified. The question now remains: what will we do about it?[47]

---

[45] *Ibid,* p.9-10.

[46] Webster's New World Dictionary, second edition, (New York, NY: Simon & Schuster, 1982), p. 1352.

[47] http://www.thedailybell.com/news-analysis/warning-government-is-in-danger-of-going-extinct/

Conclusion

As America becomes more diverse in terms of cultural patterns due to immigrants, legal or otherwise, as well as changing religious and cultural norms among the historic American population of European ancestry, the probability of societal collapse becomes more acute. It is a matter of time, demography, and daily action that will forever change the basis of unity in the American Union, making it less likely for people to feel they are part of anything on a national scale that stimulates any form of patriotism as well as the willingness to hold together and defend it. This has and will continue to cause a civilizational crisis as there is no longer a Core Values foundation for the nation to rally around and build upon for the future.

What was once the cosmopolitan mix of the peripheral areas that America had impacted abroad as it projected power, both soft and hard, has now come home to America proper. This will lead to a slow societal collapse as the politically correct social justice warriors backed up by the power of the State will force Americans to accept these changes of social norms. As can be seen by the vehemence expressed both in the media along with the streets of modern America over the past few years – this will NOT happen easily and without conflict.

Such societal conflict will not go away and in time will force the dissolution of the states in actuality rather just in terms of Core Values and social ethos which already exists. It is only a matter of time before simple economics and political problems as noted in *America's Age of Empires* impresses this upon America also as she will have less money to either go abroad militarily as well as subsidize social programs domestically which will lead to even more conflict.

The question remains – what will replace the current social order?[48]

---

[48] https://freeprivatecities.com/

The Natural Order of Human Society:

Who Shall Lead?

The "natural order" of society is both old (meaning historic) and natural (meaning self-perpetuating if left alone) rather than artificial (meaning having been based upon the new anomalies or deviance's justified by the academics of modernity and post-modernity).[49] Natural Order refers to both the natural, family

---

[49] "Out of every hundred new ideas ninety-nine or more will probably be inferior to the traditional responses which they propose to replace. No one man, however brilliant or well-informed, can come in one lifetime to such fullness of understanding as to safely judge and dismiss the customs or institutions of his society, for those are the wisdom of generations after centuries of experiment in the laboratory of history." Thomas Sowell, *The Vision of the Anointed*, (Basic Books: New York; 1995), p. 112.

based formation of societies,[50] as well as the inescapable reality that some people are naturally endowed by their Creator with certain talents and abilities (Dan.1:4; Matt.25:14-15; I Pet.4:11) that allow them to excel above and beyond the norm.

In other words, certain people will arise in society naturally to positions of social prominence, achieving prosperity and success through their individual

---

[50] "But thought can stop short of ultimates and yet grasp the natural law existence of communities and their orders. For the ontological necessity of, say, the family, nationality, occupational group, and state clearly results from the idea of man, not from the idea of the state. The national community, which is built up through the community of blood, language, and culture (national spirit) out of families (basically therefore upon biological being, and not upon the *nomos*), is also prior to the state, even though it may tend toward the form of statehood and may be on the way to becoming a state. But nation and state do not coincide conceptually: as there is a national state, so there is a non-national or multi-national state. Furthermore, inside the national economy and culture the members of the nation are organized according to their professional function into occupational groups, and according to locality into political groups, for the complete achievement of the common good." Heinrich A. Rommen, *The Natural Law*, (Liberty Fund, Indianapolis, IN., 1998), p. 211.

intellectual, physical and social labor if they are educated according to their natural predispositions.

The question remains, however, how does one go about developing such an "order"? Or, does the "order" result naturally if people are allowed freedom rather than being managed from womb to tomb by the agency of the State and its myriad of social service workers, university and media thought-police, or psychologists for the purpose of a *secular* attempt at social engineering[51] through law similar to Aristotle.[52] Indeed, Aristotle, similar to his

---

[51] "Modern anthropology defines man in abstraction from God and in terms of an evolving cosmos which is a product of chance. Modern man defines himself in terms of his own "autonomous" will and desire, and he regards life and the universe as evil if he is not satisfied with his self-fulfillment. For theology to concentrate on man's being, and to seek to define man apart from his creation and calling, is to fall into the same kind of abstraction. We have an abstract and therefore false definition of man whenever and wherever man is not viewed in his totality in terms of God's calling." R.J. Rushdoony, *Systematic Theology,* (Vallecito, CA: Ross House Books, 1994), *Vol.2,* p. 903-4.

mentor Plato, had strong opinions as to what an "order" was, and how it should be set up and maintained.[53]

In the section to follow, we will consider the question of the development of the natural order versus the current artificial order of society. We will begin by looking at what currently is the case in modern America. From there we will move on to what could be the case if people are willing to return to the foundations of the past.

Does Famous = Worthy of Praise?

[52] In Aristotle's mind, man's chief end was moral and intellectual contemplation and virtue lived within community with others. He believed that the purpose of political action was to make men virtuous. See: Aristotle, *Politics,* Trans. B. Jowett; *Historical Introduction to Philosophy,* ed. Albert B. Hakim, 4th edition, (New Jersey: Prentice Hall, 2001), 1:2. See also Aristotle, *Nichomachean Ethics,* 2:1103b.3-5 wherein he wrote, "for legislators make the citizens good by forming habits in them."

[53] Aristotle's *Politics,* 1:1-6; Plato's *Republic,* discussions on "cities as soul" (443d-e), one man, one job, the right man for the right job minding his own business (433a-b), virtue ruling the city (431d-432a), and the city being ruled by the best and brightest (428e-429a).

One only has to look at the current leaders of society, both politically as well as culturally in the areas of the arts, music and sports to see people looked to for their opinions in print or on the screen for no other reason than they are rich, famous and/or beautiful rather than intelligent, hardworking and morally upright.[54] Even

54 "As we move toward the next century, a high proportion of people in the growing cognitive elite have been given little religious or moral education in the family. The commonest religion of the elite is an agnostic humanism. Many such families are themselves split by divorce, remarriage, and subsequent third marriages. The marriage pattern in Hollywood [who produce our "culture" via videos and movies – ERS] is not universal in the United States, but the cognitive elite in Euro-America has a high divorce rate, probably averaging a third or more. The children of these divorced parents seldom have a basic religious education, and are aware of the variations of moral attitude between parents, stepparents, and stepsiblings. If one compares the initial moral education of this group with that of an Irish or Polish village, the peasant education obviously provides much the stronger religious training of the two. A godless, rootless, and rich elite is unlikely to be happy or to be loved. This inadequacy in the initial moral education of what will be the dominant economic group of the next century is likely to be reinforced by their life

more problematic is the fact that people in society generally want to follow after these cultural "leaders" if for no other reason than they are "rich, famous and/or

---

experience. These people will have the discipline of an advanced technical education, of one sort or another, to fit themselves for their new role as the leaders of the new electronic universe. But they will learn from that only some of the moral lessons that have historically been the framework for human social conduct. By the standards of Confucius, Buddha, or Plato (500 B.C.), St. Paul (A.D. 50), or Mahomet (A.D. 600), they may be morally illiterates. They will have been taught the lessons of economic efficiency, the use of resources, the pursuit of money, but not the virtues of humility or self-sacrifice, let alone chastity. Essentially most of them will have been brought up as pagans with a set of values closer to those of the late Roman Republic than to Christianity. Even these values will be highly individualistic, rather than shared. Societies, as we have argued, can only be strong if real moral values are widely shared. The advanced nations are already moving into the situation where many people will hold weak or limited moral values, others will compensate with fierce adherence to irrational values, and few values will be held in common across the whole of society." James Dale Davidson & Lord Rees-Mogg, *The Sovereign Individual,* (New York, NY: Simon & Schuster, 1997), p. 367.

beautiful" as opposed to "intelligent, hardworking and morally upright."[55]

Politically, we have cheesy elections with all the fanfare and foolishness that surrounds the various political conventions where the so-called elite are presented to

---

[55] "The return of Western culture to its pagan past bears striking correspondence to the pattern of Toynbee's typology of mimesis. He was impressed by the universal tendency to pattern cultural and economic institutions after those of other peoples. The direction of the mimesis is crucial. In primitive societies it is directed uncritically toward elders and ancestors. When a civilization is being formed, the mimetic focus shifts to creative people who command a following by reason of their pioneering activities and their accomplishments. One way to evaluate the future of a society is to determine the direction of mimesis. Who admires whom and on what grounds? Who seeks to be more like whom?... At the same time the formerly-dominant civilization begins imitating the various proletariats, the latter cease to emulate those people they formerly regarded as their betters, and return to their own once-despised traditions. In the fourth century, when the barbarians in the Roman armies began keeping their own names instead of adopting those of the Romans, the Romans, including the imperial court, began aping barbarian manners, customs, and dress. Thus, Toynbee endorsed Christopher Dawson's observation that the mark of a culture's last stage is not decay but syncretism." Herbert Schlossberg, *Idols For Destruction,* (Nashville, TN:Thomas Nelson, 1983), p. 268-9.

the world. From there, it is viscous attacks, big promises (many false from the start) and word games that make even a Shakespearean drama seem boring as they seek to be elected for offices of empire wherein, similar to the Romans of old, they live lives that are debauched (Matt.7:16), power hungry (Lk.22:25), and far removed from the reality of the common man whom they are to serve and protect. Former University of Nevada professor Hans-Hermann Hoppe illustrates this reality for us below:

> The fortunes of great families have dissipated, and their tradition of culture and economic independence, intellectual farsightedness, and moral and spiritual leadership has been forgotten. Rich men still exist today, but more frequently than not they owe their fortune now directly

or indirectly to the state. Hence, they are often more dependent on the state's continued favors than people of far lesser wealth. They are typically no longer heads of long established leading families but *nouveaux riches.* Their conduct is not marked by special virtue, dignity, or taste but is a reflection of the same proletarian mass-culture of present-orientedness, opportunism, and hedonism that the rich now share with everyone else; consequently, their opinions carry no more weight in public opinion than anyone else's.[56]

In opposition to the current status quo noted above, we desire a natural elite that would arise from amongst the community

---

[56] Hans-Herman Hoppe, *Democracy: The God That Failed,* (New Brunswick, NJ:Transaction Press, 2001), p. 73-74.

due to their own character, talents and abilities as well as their performance in the social sphere of society as benefactors.[57] Even more to the point of our discussion on the Natural Order is the necessity of a legal structure that would allow such people to naturally gain the ascendancy in society through service as Christ Himself preached was the true order of leadership that blesses all (Mark 10:42-45). In other words, this "elite" would arise naturally from the community based upon character, accomplishment and philanthropic spirit and action as opposed to the current methods unfortunately employed in both the political and business realm.

The Natural Nobility

Our purpose here is to identify a social structure that would truly be decentralized

---

[57] *But he who is noble plans noble things, and on noble things he stands (Isa.32:8;ESV).*

down to the level of the town or small city. Equally, we desire both an educational and legal system that would allow for the development of a Natural Order of occupational leadership amongst the citizens that due to their own virtue, impeccable character and natural economic ability would rise "naturally" to the top of their community rather than through political connections, government subsidy, *nouveaux riches* or judicial acts of "social justice" and the attempts at forced "equal opportunity" in the socio-economic sphere.

In the business realm and other occupational categories we would desire the same thing: experienced economic actors – not Hollywood actors and political pundits! – who through hard work and service and good reputation – rather than government approval and certification – have risen to the top of their field and may be considered the "true experts" in society as opposed to the government sanctioned, supported and enforced pretenders and their endless regulations that do more harm than good as they protect their monopoly of position and power while negating the ability of others to compete by implementing endless regulation and certification requirements. In other words, and as Wilhelm Ropke clearly states:

> What we need is true *nobilitas naturalis*. No era can do without it, least of all ours, when so much is shaking and crumbling away. We need a natural nobility whose authority is, fortunately, readily accepted by all men, an elite deriving its title solely from supreme performance and peerless moral example and invested with the moral dignity of such a life. Only a few from every stratum of

society can ascend into this thin layer of natural nobility. The way to it is an exemplary and slowly maturing life of dedicated endeavor on behalf of all, unimpeachable integrity, constant restraint of our common greed, proved soundness of judgment, a spotless private life, indomitable courage in standing up for truth and law, and generally the highest example. This is how the few, carried upward by the trust of the people, gradually attain to a position above the classes, interests, passions, wickedness, and foolishness of men and finally become the nation's conscience. To belong to this group of moral aristocrats should be the highest and most desirable aim, next to which all the other triumphs of life are pale and insipid... no free society, least of all ours, which threatens to degenerate into mass society, can subsist without such a class of censors. The continued existence of our free world will ultimately depend on whether our age can produce a sufficient number of such aristocrats of public spirit.[58]

The purpose behind such an ethos amongst the leadership of society is to allow human-beings to do that which they were created by God to do: steward the owner's resources (Gen.1:26-28). In order to fulfill their task as an actor in history, they must have freedom of choice that will allow them to act freely in their dominion task (Gen.1:26-28) without interference by others whether an individual or group such as the government. This will allow for the natural development of individual talents

---

[58] Wilhelm Ropke, *A Humane Economy,* (Indianapolis, Ind.: Liberty Fund, 1971), p. 130-131.

and abilities on both an individual and corporate level which will allow for the development of civilization that in turn will reflect the talents and abilities of the citizens within it as they attain even higher levels of progress.

In other words, it must be understood from the start that each individual must be viewed as a true sovereign actor in history with the freedom to morally act out his stewardship to whatever level he chooses as long as he does not interfere with the life, liberty and property of other actors. Herein lies the importance of both leadership and a legal system that will protect individuals, their property, and their personal stewardship of both from interference by others.

It is only with the understanding of and agreement with these foundational principles that a truly free and prosperous society can arise and survive long-term as men and women seek to fulfill their purpose on earth before God and for God – rather than for the benefit of the State and its internal bureaucracies who utilize money taxed from productive people and given to others "less fortunate"[59] thus starting the process of decivilization[60] that always occurs when the best and the brightest (i.e. the natural aristocrats) are burdened with subsidizing the masses.[61]

Decentralized City-States

On a civilizational level, the ultimate purpose of our educational and occupational pursuits is the developing of decentralized city-states that will,

---

[59] Consider the following anthology on the affect of religion on culture in the book *Culture Matters: How Values Shape Human Progress,* a symposium edited by Lawrence E. Harrison and Samuel P. Huntington, (New York, NY: Basic Books, 2000), pages 24, 47-48, 52, 87-91, 104-107, 111, 119, 120-122.

[60] *Democracy: The God That Failed*, Chapter One.

[61] Thomas Sowell, *The Quest for Cosmic Justice,* (New York, NY: The Free Press, 1999).

according to *Plowing In Hope* author David Hegeman, ring the globe as a garland of garden cites to the glory of God:

> God's intent is that nature, man-made structures, and well-crafted artifacts be married together into a glorious, harmonious whole. It is important for us to recapture the biblical vision of the garden-city – a global network of cities, park-lands, agricultural fields and groves, forests and wilderness preserves – as the goal of mankind's culturative activities. The garden-city points to the necessity of a well-developed community to achieve culturative success. The glory of the heavenly Jerusalem implies that the culturative development of the earth will have a considerable richness and scope. This will only be possible as significant numbers of people, blessed with diverse gifts and skills, live and work together toward a common, God-

defined end. Where do men and women live together in significant numbers so that this noble end may be reached? The city! The city is both the means and the goal of our culturative calling before God. The garden is only the starting point. The garden-city also implies that there is to be harmony between humans and nature, that the works of man and the works of nature are both vital and are both to co-exist and complement one another.[62]

If we consider the writings of the Old Testament prophet Micah, along with the other examples of the relationship between believers and people in power, we do not see "empire" as the apex of the "good life" for the man of God but quite the opposite (Micah 4:1-5).

Along similar lines of thought, we equally do not see human beings managed

---

[62] David Bruce Hegeman, *Plowing In Hope,* (Moscow, ID: Canon Press, 1999), p. 35.

by the State from womb to tomb. Thus, we should obviously understand that all forms of fascism, socialism and communism are morally wrong as they remove the possibility of personal stewardship before God as the *imago Dei*. Equally of note, and as has been seen before in history, is the danger of right-wing Statism that contains within it the same tendencies as the above mentioned "isms" regarding the monopolization of both power and force and the tendency to project that force in acts of social engineering domestically, and imperialism internationally. In either case, human beings are forced to be an agent for the State with dire consequences for human nature in the realm of physical, psychological, emotional and social well-being (I Sam.8:10-18). Subsequently, these negative effects spread to overall society and the ability of human beings to live free and develop a civilization according to their individual talents and abilities, all the while caring for themselves and their families; the basis of human society.[63]

Foundations

Our next consideration is obvious: What foundation, sociologically speaking, do we need to enact that would allow the above vision to develop and flourish?

Once again, if we consider the writings of the Old Testament prophet Micah, we do not see "empire" as the apex of the "good life" for the man of God but quite the opposite (Micah 4:1-5). Indeed, we see a decentralized order of man as the owner/steward of his property under God, living without fear as he fulfills his original dominion task (Gen.1:26-28). From there we see the progression of mankind into the social unit of the family as the next structure God used to order his creation (Gen.2:24). These were relationships of kin

---

[63] *The Natural Law*, p. 211.

both nuclear and extended that expanded outward through marriage and positive birthrate along with domestic servants and wanderers attaching themselves to these patriarchal groups as in the case of Abraham and later the Israelites as a people as they slowly evolved into a nation (Genesis 6:18; 14:14; 11:31; 36:39; Ex.18:21-23; 31:2,6).

What is instructive about this evolution from wandering patriarchs who headed up families that eventually became clans and tribes and finally a nation was the governing structure that was based upon birth, moral and social authority as well as ability (Ex.18:19-23).

In the past, local governments were designated as "towns." Every town (literally, "gate") had its own court system with its own rulers and administrators. Affairs of the towns were to be handled by the officials of the town selected "out of all the people" from the town (Deut.16:18).

Local affairs were to be handled by the "elders of the city" because those who ruled are known by the people: "Her husband is known in the gates, when he sits among the elders of the land" (Prov. 31:23). In other words, all leaders were also husbands and fathers and ruled with an attitude and practice of humble stewardship as Augustine noted long ago:

> But those who are true fathers of their households desire and endeavor that all the members of their household, equally with their own children, should worship and win God, and should come to that heavenly home in which the duty of ruling men is no longer necessary, because the duty of caring for their everlasting happiness has also ceased; but, until they reach that home, masters ought to feel their position of authority a greater burden than servants their service. And if any member of the family interrupts the domestic peace by

disobedience, he is corrected either by
word or blow, or some kind of just and
legitimate punishment, such as society
permits, that he may himself be the
better for it, and be readjusted to the
family harmony from which he had
dislocated himself. For as it is not
benevolent to give a man help at the
expense of some greater benefit he
might receive, so it is not innocent to
spare a man at the risk of his falling into
graver sin. To be innocent, we must not
only do harm to no man, but also
restrain him from sin or punish his sin,
so that either the man himself who is
punished may profit by his experience,
or others be warned by his example.
Since, then, the house ought to be the
beginning or element of the city, and
every beginning bears reference to some
end of its own kind, and every element
to the integrity of the whole of which it
is an element, it follows plainly enough
that domestic peace has a relation to

civic peace --in other words, that the well-ordered concord of domestic obedience and domestic rule has a relation to the well-ordered concord of civic obedience and civic rule. And therefore it follows, further, that the father of the family ought to frame his domestic rule in accordance with the law of the city, so that the household may be in harmony with the civic order.[64]

As R.J. Rushdoony notes: "Elders formed the basis of civil government. Since men who governed in so extensive a fashion their own households were best trained to govern, Moses turned to the elders, at the command of God, to form a group of seventy to rule Israel (Num. 11:16). These men governed under Moses and aided him in instructing the people in the implications of the law (Deut.27:1). Local

___

[64] *City of God,* XIX.xvi.

government was in the hands of elders (Deut.19:12; 21:2; 22:15; 25:7; Josh.[4:4]; Judges 8:14; Ruth 4:2). These elders are also referred to in the Gospels (Matt.16:21; 26:47; Luke 7:3)."[65]

The above paradigm can be further illustrated by pointing to some very specific essentials as far as what it takes sociologically to make the internal *ethos* of a city, thus the social structure of the city itself vibrant and flourishing because it allows for the *spontaneous* development of a society. Hoppe illustrates this principle in his schema for conservative social structure for us below:

> Conservative refers to someone who recognized the old and natural through the "noise" of anomalies and accidents and who defends, supports, and helps to preserve it against the temporary and

---

[65] R.J. Rushdoony, *Institutes of Biblical Law,* (Vallecito, CA: Ross House Books, 1973), *Vol.1,* p. 740.

anomalous. Within the realm of the humanities, including the social sciences, a conservative recognizes families (fathers, mothers, children, grandchildren) and households based on private property and in cooperation with a community of other households as the most fundamental, natural, essential, ancient, and indispensable social units. Moreover, the family household also represents the model of the social order at large. Just as a hierarchical order exists in a family, so is there a hierarchical order within a community of families – of apprentices, servants, and masters, vassals, knights, lords, overlords, and even kings – tied together by an elaborate and intricate system of kinship relations; and of children, parents, priests, and bishops and finally the transcendent God. Of the two layers of authority, the earthly physical power of parents, lords, and kings is naturally subordinate and subject to control by the ultimate spiritual-intellectual authority of father, priests, bishops and ultimately God.[66]

Relationally, or perhaps better put, *sociologically,* the paragraph by Hoppe above gives us something to aim toward regarding the symbiotic nature of a biblical or "conservative" society in terms of peaceful human interaction. Equally of note is the interlocking and counter-balancing nature of all those different levels that, reminiscent of the medieval city-states, act as a restraint against runaway power that we currently face in a centralized societal structure.

By implication, we should consider the same paradigm: localism at a greatly decentralized level compared to the current paradigm modern Americans live under. Although having memorized the traditions

---

[66] *Democracy: The God That Failed,* p. 188.

of the past and believing the political rhetoric of the present, most Americans are generally oblivious to their true financial and legal plight under the modern super-state America has become and the cascading effects of a humanistic worldview. [67]

Upon reflecting on this dilemma, perhaps the real problem for those outside the Christian community is both the silence of the Church in many areas, and its lack of clarity and consistency in its message. Unless the Church, as "the ground and pillar of the truth"(1 Tim.3:15) does its job prophetically according to Scripture (2 Tim.3:16-17) there will be no basis for truth

---

[67] Charolette Twight, *Dependent on D.C.*, (New York, NY: Palgrave, 2002). Indeed, 4th century Church Father Augustine was concerned about the danger in allowing a city to grow too big due to the difficulty of not only managing it, but the tendency of rulers to grasp for more and more power, and the desire to project this "power" on neighboring cities or countries. See: Augustine, *City of God,* Trans. Henry Bettenson, (London, England: Penguin Books, 1972; 1984), IV.xv.

(Col.2:8-10) thus leaving man in a state of intellectual and moral free-fall (Gal.6:7). This must change, because at the heart of this dilemma is the key to the large global debate over what constitutes a "good society" thus a "good culture" for the human being. Moreover, that "key" is the issue of a Christian world and life view, and the ability to reconcile religion with society based upon a solid foundation of faith in a transcendent being (God) yet utilizing principles that will provide opportunities for unity rather than fragmentation which is normally the case now.

It will be this reconciliation and the application of the subsequent principles that will provide the foundation upon which a society shall understand what a human being is, how they are to live and be governed in relation to God, people, places and things as well as what their purpose in life should be (Matt.4:4; 7:24-29).

Conclusion

The "Natural Order" refers to the inescapable reality that some people are naturally endowed by their Creator with certain talents and abilities that allow them to excel above and beyond the norm. In other words, certain people will arise in society naturally to positions of social prominence, achieving prosperity and success through their own individual intellectual, physical and social labor if they are educated according to their natural predispositions and left alone by the State. Their efforts will in turn be a blessing to those within their community both in action and testimony.

Parents, pastors and educators must bear in mind that their goal is *not* to educate the children committed to their trust to be absorbed into modern American mass culture and "find a job." Rather, they are to assist young people in finding out who and what they are under God co-relative to their talents and abilities so that they are able raise up and rebuild the Republic.

Granted, this is a multi-generational endeavor that grows over time but it generally begins with one person, male or female that achieves excellence above and beyond the norm and raises their children to hold on to the vision, and influences the community accordingly.[68] With proper training and constant reinforcement of the vision as "our vision" it is understood as a community that this is what "we" do to maintain continuity with those who have gone before us. To do otherwise is to accept the current social situation as

---

[68] Adam Bellow, *In Praise of Nepotism*, (Doubleday Books:New York, 2003), p. 465.

normal, all the while ignoring the results that have and will occur (Gal.6:7).

Can something like this be possible given the current structure of the American mega-state and its international "concerns"? Equally, what legal standard do we enact to protect the above?

City States: Small & Independent

There are three essential examples available to consider in a fairly expedient fashion: Free State; City State & Charter Colony. They are all examples of localized government, yet they all have different governing structures to consider prior to choosing one as opposed to the other. For example, the most "free" from outside interference of any kind is the "City State." Simply defined, as city state is:

> A **City-State** is a sovereign state consisting of a city and its dependent territories. Historically this included famous cities like Rome, Athens, Carthage and the Italian city-states during the

Renaissance, but today only a handful of sovereign city-states exist, with some disagreement as to which states should and should not be considered as city-states. However, a great deal of consensus exists that the term properly applies to Singapore, Monaco and Vatican City. Other states that often get cited as being modern city-states include Malta, San Marino, Liechtenstein, Andorra, Luxemburg, Qatar, Brunei, Kuwait and Bahrain.[69]

A city-state is a country, however small, which is beholden to none. It is thoroughly sovereign over its own affairs and in all areas that a country exists: government, legal, educational, economical, medical, social norms and

---

overall culture sensibilities. An interesting feature about all such city states historically (i.e. Tyre & Carthage) and presently is that they are generally centers for banking, finance, trade or administration of international organizations (i.e. Vatican City). Free States, as the definition below will show, are essentially the same.

> **Free State** is a term occasionally used in the official titles of some states. In *principle* the title asserts and emphasizes the freedom of the state in question, but what this actually means varies greatly in different contexts: Sometimes it asserts sovereignty or independence (and with that, lack of foreign domination). Sometimes it asserts autonomy within a larger nation-state. Sometimes it is used as a synonym for republic but not all

"free states" have been republics. While the historical German free states and the Orange Free State were republican in form, the Congo and Irish Free States were governed under forms of monarchy. In this essay, "Free State" or "Free City" will refer to an organization similar to an independent entity — sometimes called a "city state" whose territory consists of a city which is not administered as part of another local government. Although some "free states" are, similar to "city states," completely free and sovereign entities, many are located within, and at the prerogative of a still larger nation-state. Examples of city states would be: Hong Kong [sadly this has changed] and Macau, along with independent members of the United Arab Emirates, most notably Dubai and Abu Dhabi, often are cited as such.[70]

Granted, there can be a multitude of reasons for such socio-political entities to exist. Generally, they exist due to some type of charter or treaty that has been made between two political entities. In the case of both Hong Kong and Macau, these territories were seized by European powers centuries ago and used as colonies to enrich the mother countries in various forms of mercantilism. In time, however, although still "colonies," they were allowed to exist as both "windows to the world" and "trading centers" outside of Communist China legally, yet still on Chinese soil geographically. Both have since been "returned" to China – the real "mother country" – yet they still function as they did

---

70
https://en.wikipedia.org/wiki/Free_state_(governme
nt)

economically when under European powers as centers of trade, finance and various forms of investment and tourism, yet maintaining a distance between the other citizens of mainland China.

A similar situation exists with the United Arab Emirates wherein they are located along the Arabian Peninsula and clearly part of Saudi Arabia geographically, yet separate and distinct politically. Historically, they also were either under the control of, or highly influenced by European countries, yet for various reasons (and unlike Hong Kong and Macau), remained independent rather than become an actual "colony." Similar also to Hong Kong and Macau, they are involved in trade and finance as well as oil, which brings in tremendous revenue. The seven separate emirates are independent of Saudi Arabia yet have trade relationships and act, in many respects considering the size of their expatriate population, as a window to the world for the Arabian Peninsula yet still maintaining their cultural sensibilities in terms of religion, morals and legal structure. Each emirate is ruled by a monarch with one of the monarchs acting as president for their federation called "The United Arab Emirates."

Lastly are the concepts from America's past: the Charter Colony, Proprietary Colony and the Royal Colony:

> **Charter Colony:** was specifically governed by a trade company (such as the Virginia Company) that received its authorization from the king. Charter colonies usually enjoyed the most independence in their government.

> **Proprietary Colony:** under this arrangement, the king appointed a

proprietor or proprietors (ultimately responsible to the king) to govern a colony.

Royal Colony: these colonies were controlled directly by the crown, which meant that the king and his councilors appointed the governor directly.

By the seventeenth century a number of charter and proprietary colonies had become royal colonies as the king assumed increasing control over colonial affairs. From there, of course, came the War for American Independence followed by victory and the Articles of Confederation, the Constitution, and America as it is now known and governed as both a continental and world-wide superpower, mega-state.

Which Structure is Best?

A discussion of the city and the ordering of community life within it is a daunting task. Where do we begin our conversation, and how do we frame the discussion so as to prevent getting bogged down in all the details and theories of what a city, and "city life" is all about?

This question is not as difficult as it seems if we are willing to think outside the box of what America *currently* is and consider what has existed in the past both domestically and internationally yet with a twist in the sense of having learned – hopefully! – lessons from history.

What history has shown us is that sooner or later, all governmental structures beyond a certain size are prone to dissolution over time due to the necessity of time, money, effort and blood to hold them together beyond a certain geographical area (Acts 17:26). Indeed, history is the story of how nations rise and fall due to either being conquered by other nations or marauding people groups[71] or through over-extending themselves to the point of exhaustion (when the State cannot pay the legions, they always come home, thus ending their international activities. Bottom-line: minus major economic and political changes on the home front – you end up with regime collapse and the end of the old order).

Regardless of personal preference or hopes, it is only a matter of time before America as we currently know it changes into something most of us will not recognize. The question then will be: given that all centralized orders in time collapse – what will come about next? Equally of note, will that "what" be something that was thought through ahead of time or something cobbled together *ad hoc*?

---

[71] Thomas Sowell, *Conquests and Cultures*, (Basic Books: New York, 1998).

Assuming we would want something with staying power and beyond a short-term *ad hoc* solution, the present would be the best time to consider such a move, so let us begin by suggesting the "free state" model. In the ultimate sense, the goal should be to aim toward a "city state" model to allow individuals to develop their own Natural Order wherein they could flourish regardless of their religious perspective.

On a civilizational level, and once again from the Christian perspective, the ultimate purpose of our socio-political pursuits would be the developing of city-states that will, according to *Plowing In Hope* author David Hegeman, ring the globe as a garland of garden cites to the glory of God:

> God's intent is that nature, man-made structures, and well-crafted artifacts be married together into a glorious, harmonious whole. It is important for

us to recapture the biblical vision of the garden-city – a global network of cities, park-lands, agricultural fields and groves, forests and wilderness preserves – as the goal of mankind's culturative activities. The garden-city points to the necessity of a well-developed community to achieve culturative success. The glory of the heavenly Jerusalem implies that the culturative development of the earth will have a considerable richness and scope. This will only be possible as significant numbers of people, blessed with diverse gifts and skills, live and work together toward a common, God-defined end. Where do men and women live together in significant numbers so that this noble end may be reached? The city! The city is both the means and the goal of our culturative calling before God. The garden is only the starting point. The garden-city also implies that there is to be harmony between humans and nature, that the works of man and the works of nature are both vital and are both to co-exist and complement one another. If we consider the writings of the Old Testament prophet Micah, along with the other examples of the relationship between believers and people in power, we do not see "empire" as the apex of the "good life" for the man of God but quite the opposite (Micah 4:1-5).

Within those cities noted in the above quote would be the understanding that a city would be self-contained in context of its *internal ethos*. The inner-workings for a biblical city are similar to an ordinary city in terms of city planning, infrastructure, population growth, economics and socio-political activity as well as the everyday dynamics of buying, selling, worship, living and dying and all in accordance to a similar hope for the future: peace and the common good life as biblical scholar R.J. Rushdoony suggests below:

> The city represents a common life. From the earliest days, the function of the city has been to provide men with community, to bring like-minded men together in terms of a common purpose and life. The city served as an expanded family. Men felt "at home" in their city, because it represented a large family and a closely knit sense of community. This aspect of the city is now gone. Instead of a sense of belonging, the city gives a sense of isolation. The word "citizenship" comes from the word "city"; citizenship was originally membership in the common life and faith of a city. Instead of citizenship, modern man finds instead alienation in the city.[72]

---

[72] R.J. Rushdoony, *Roots of Reconstructionism,* "Chalcedon Report No.61; September 1, 1970" (Vallecito, CA: Ross House Books, 1991), p. 718.

Granted, there are differences between a biblically oriented city or town and that of your ordinary "secular" city that can be broken down into something specific that is needed to make the *internal ethos* of a city itself cohesive. In other words, regardless of whether someone lives in a city that is faith oriented or secular, either a city seeks some common ground as a point of unity or it inescapably ends up with fragmentation sociologically. To be sure, there are many factors that can be attributed to both the concepts and reality of unity and fragmentation that are beyond the scope of this essay. Nonetheless, and in terms of living space and community development, a well thought-through moral and legal plan, philosophically speaking will act as a template or paradigm of how a group of people will live and interact together as they live out their life in context of a local community, whether urban or rural.

Therefore, in context of our present situation here in America, living within the current social-political structure of the United States, a "free state" would be the best model to follow initially as it allows for change at not only a gradual level, but equally an inevitable one as more states seek to enact legal principles of nullification regarding Federal Laws believed to be unconstitutional according to the 10th Amendment.

Although there are a multitude of principles that need to be worked through, what needs to be understood first and foremost is the idea of Free States as competing jurisdictions which seek to encourage the emigration of talented, self-governed people of similar background and world life views into areas wherein they can live and work together.[73] These jurisdictions would operate according to a

---

[73] https://mises.org/blog/just-boundaries-and-national-self-determination

social contract or covenant wherein people agree to abide by a series of laws that reconcile the individual's desire for freedom with the rule of law; yet "law" as all would agree upon in advance to be acceptable, as opposed to the current situation wherein the government *is a monopoly of force* which it can project at will. As discussed in *The Sovereign Individual,* people would come to realize:

> What we now think of as "political" leadership, which is always conceived in terms of a nation-state, will become increasingly entrepreneurial rather than political in nature. In these conditions, the viable range of choice in putting together a "policy" regime for a jurisdiction will be effectively narrowed in the same way that the range of options open to entrepreneurs in designing a first-class resort hotel or any similar product or service is defined by what people will pay for. A

resort hotel, for example would seldom attempt to operate on terms that required guests to perform hard labor to repair and extend its facilities. Even a resort hotel owned or controlled by its employees, like the typical modern democracy, would try in vain to force customers to comply with such demands, especially after better accommodations became available. If the customers would rather play golf than do heavy labor in the hot sun, then on that question, at least, the market offers little scope for imposing arbitrary alternatives. In such conditions, presently "political" issues will recede into entrepreneurial judgments, as jurisdictions seek to discover what policy bundles will attract customers.[74]

The implications of the above is staggering in a world wherein people still

---

[74] *The Sovereign Individual*, p. 329.

refer to their nation-state as "their country" in spite of the fact that they have no real control of their economy, legal system, or bank accounts. The whole idea that people would walk away (as various individuals have for nearly twenty years now) in search of a better domicile with safe streets, law taxes and minimal governmental intrusion is unfathomable no matter what invasive domestic policies have been enacted since 9/11 by the Bush regime and Obama Care under the current regime. People have been trained to think that because they can cast a vote once every four years they are truly free.

Equally part of that training (indoctrination?) is the refusal to consider a different perspective on the current configuration of the United States. In the end, as has been the case throughout history when civilizations have over-extended themselves to Quigley's third level, collapse always comes. There are too many divisions in modern America that will prevent a true, heartfelt unity from developing again without a sea-change in world and life view and psycho-spiritual-moral commitments. There is no basis for a union that people are willing to commit themselves outside of personal self-interest.

Outside the Current Box

The future will be different as many will view loyalty not attached to a bygone era of a nation-state but rather to principles of shared values including privacy, protection and freedom which they will negotiate for in an independent fashion within "competitive territorial clubs" rather than allow these principles to be at the mercy of politicians.[75] The concept of protection versus extortion will be carefully thought through by citizens of such "clubs" as they will not be interested in living under

---

[75] *Ibid*, p. 334-335.

coercive tax policies wherein they have to support anyone beyond their own families, or pay property tax for schools their children do not attend.

Consider the rise of the gated community but on a much larger scale minus the multiple tax liabilities that those living within them currently face in the United States. Indeed, "Any government that insists upon lumbering its citizens with heavy taxes that competitors do not pay will merely assure that profits and wealth gravitate somewhere else. Therefore, the failure of the mature welfare states to curtail taxes over the long term will be self-correcting. Governments that tax too much will simply make residence anywhere within their power a bankrupting liability."[76]

People will vote with their feet and leave the current warfare/welfare state

---

[76] *Ibid,* p. 196.

behind as settlers from the old world left Europe five hundred years ago for a "new world." What will our "new world" look like?

Consider the following reference to the Middle Ages in Europe and fast forward to our time:

> You will also see the re-emergence of associations of merchants and wealthy individuals with semi-sovereign powers, like the Hanse (confederation of merchants) in the Middle Ages. The Hanse that operated in the French and Flemish fairs grew to encompass the merchants of sixty cities. The "Hanseatic League," as it is redundantly known in English (the literal translation is "Leaguely League"), was an organization of Germanic merchant guilds that provided protection to members and

negotiated trade treaties. It came to exercise semi-sovereign powers in a number of Northern European and Baltic cities. Such entities will re-emerge in place of the dying nation-state in the new millennium, providing protection and helping to enforce contracts in an unsafe world.

In short, the future is likely to confound the expectations of those who have absorbed the civic myths of twentieth-century industrial society. Among them are the illusions of social democracy that once thrilled and motivated the most gifted minds. They presuppose that societies evolve in whatever way governments wish them to – preferably in response to opinion polls and scrupulously counted votes. This was never as true as it seemed fifty years ago. Now it is an anachronism, as much an artifact of industrialism as a rusting smokestack. The civic myths reflect not only a mindset that sees society's problems as susceptible to engineering solutions: they also reflect a false confidence that resources and individuals will remain as vulnerable to political compulsion in the future as they have been in the twentieth century. We doubt it. Market forces, not political majorities, will compel societies to reconfigure themselves in ways public opinion will neither comprehend nor welcome. As they do, the naïve view that history is what people wish it to be will prove wildly misleading.

It will therefore be crucial that you see the world anew. That means looking from the outside in to reanalyze much that you have probably taken for granted. This will enable you to come to a new understanding. If you fail to transcend conventional thinking at a time when conventional thinking is losing touch with reality, then you will be more likely to fall prey to an epidemic of disorientation that lies ahead. Disorientation breeds mistakes that could threaten your business, your investments, and your way of life.[77]

The above seems far-fetched, but is it really? We have chosen the idea of a "free state" to consider in our city of the future because generally speaking, most of them

____

[77] *Ibid,* p.25-26.

historically were located within a kingdom or part of an empire but were governed by a special treaty or charter that allowed them to function at an autonomous level in comparison to the governing entity that their territory was domiciled within. The same reality already exists within the United States!

Consider the fact that Texas has no state income tax; couple that with Arkansas, which has no property tax. Now combine both and you have the city of Texarkana which if you are a resident there – you pay neither state income tax nor property tax! This reality is similar to the old frontier or marsh areas that existed during the Middle Ages wherein sovereignties blended together and within that "blended" area freedom existed above and beyond the neighboring territories located strictly within the borders of

countries,[78] or in the case noted above –
neighboring states.

In the modern world as noted earlier in
discussions on free states and city states we
see the same reality existing in Europe,
Asia, the Middle East and America in terms
of competing banking, tax and legal
jurisdictions and outright enclaves.[79]
Consider:

North American Hemisphere:
Washington D.C.;[80] Indian
Tribes;[81] Antigua and Barbuda;

---

[78] "Because of the competitive position of the two
authorities, residents of march regions seldom paid
tax. What is more, they usually had a choice in
deciding whose laws they were to obey, a choice
that was exercised through such legal concepts as
"avowal" and "distraint" that have now all but
vanished. We expect such concepts to become a
prominent feature of the law of Information
Societies." *Ibid,* p. 24.
[79] http://en.wikipedia.org/wiki/Enclave_and_exclave
[80] Washington DC has it's own tax rates:
http://www.bankrate.com/finance/taxes/state-taxes-washington-d-c.aspx

Bahamas; Belize; Bermuda; British Virgin Islands; Cayman Islands; Panama; Guam; Wake Island and 41 Independent Cities;[82] and State Income Tax Free States: Alaska; Florida; Nevada; New Hampshire; South Dakota; Tennessee; Texas; Washington & Wyoming.[83]

---

[81] "The whole course of judicial decision on the nature of Indian tribal powers is marked by adherence to three fundamental principles: An Indian tribe possesses, in the first instance, all the powers of any sovereign State. Conquest renders the tribe subject to the legislative power of the United States, and, in substance, terminates the external powers of sovereignty of the tribe, e.g., its power to enter into treaties with foreign nations, but does not by itself affect the internal sovereignty of the tribe, i.e., its powers of local self-government. These powers are subject to be qualified by treaties and by express legislation of Congress, but save as thus expressly qualified, full powers of internal sovereignty are vested in the Indian tribes and in their duly constituted organs of government." Bruce Fein, "The Last Enclaves of Banking Freedom," http://www.huffingtonpost.com/bruce-fein/the-last-enclaves-of-bank_b_1067265.html

[82] http://en.wikipedia.org/wiki/Independent_city_(United_States)

[83] http://en.wikipedia.org/wiki/State_income_tax

European Hemisphere: Vatican City; City of London within London; Liechtenstein; Andorra; Luxembourg; Switzerland; Malta; Monaco; San Marino; Channel Islands and the Isle of Man.

Middle East: United Arab Emirates; Abu Dhabi; Dubai; Qatar; Bahrain & Kuwait.

Asia: Hong Kong; Macau; Brunei & Singapore.

The point of the above list of political entities is this: with the exception of the Tax Free States along with the forty one Independent Cities located within the United States that have slightly different governing structures compared to other cities that are actually a part of the county they resided within, the majority of the other territories exist as enclaves within, or territories attached to other more powerful political entities yet maintain varying levels of autonomy in the true "free state" fashion found in the Middle Ages. Culturally they are similar to the countries nearby; yet politically, legally and financially they differ.

Equally important is the fact that the vast majority of these territories are as financially prosperous as they are politically free. That, and they are not involved in either territorial disputes or international policing operations abroad thus setting themselves up to be hated and conspired against.

Question: in as much as people gravitate to these prosperous areas to live and do business with other like-minded people – what is to stop others from doing likewise? Who would not want to live in an area wherein people are free from all forms of political paternalism and live only in accordance with the rules of engagement agreed upon in advance of their domiciling in that area?

Lastly, what is to stop a global movement toward such a reality but major governments and those who depend upon such governments for their livelihood such as bureaucrats, government contractors, tax collectors and tax/welfare recipients?

Answer: only the above-named group of people. Who else would not want to live free?

Conclusion

When we consider the reality of what the above implies, and the possibility of different jurisdictions or tax treaties, a whole new world opens up to us in our inquiry into the future structure of societies.

Conversely, when we consider that the vast majority of people who approve of the current system of centralization are either clueless as to how it operates, or benefit from it by either a government job or government handout – we should not be surprised. As Machiavelli noted in his book *The Prince* long ago, most people are concerned with appearances, as if they are reality. In time they come to believe the appearance is reality[84] and continue on as if the opposite were in fact true.

Yet the cold hard facts are that our current system of government is an incredible bureaucracy and apparatus that

---

[84] *The Prince*, Chapter 18.

looks after its own interest and the maintenance of its own power. Similar to all such expensive institutions, the law of diminishing returns sets in and more actually becomes less as the immutable laws of cause and effect set in and decivilization occurs[85] along with bankruptcy, anarchy, and fragmentation and that which was once large becomes small. It is an old pattern that has occurred from time immemorial (Dan.2) as do all such centralized systems that fly in the face of the Creator (Gen.11).

Therefore, in order to facilitate such a move toward a "free state" status, and eventually the status of an actual city state, the issue of Social Contract or Covenant will be discussed in the next chapter. What

---

[85] "The state — a judicial monopoly — must be recognized as the source of de-civilization: states do not create law and order; they destroy it." Hans-Hermann Hoppe, "The Rise and Fall of the City," November 23, 2005. See: http://mises.org/library/rise-and-fall-city

are "the rules of engagement agreed upon in advance of their domiciling in that area"? It is this discussion, and the implications of it that set the future apart from the past in context of the current political mindset yet not, as noted above, from historical realities in the distant past, nor what is already occurring domestically in the United States in some areas.

Natural Order & Social Covenants:
Nuts & Bolts

Currently we have in America a political system that philosophically is based (knowingly or not) and accepted by the American public (knowingly or not), upon the view of English philosopher Thomas Hobbes. Hobbes essentially believed that man lived within the state of nature and would kill one another unless people agreed to give up their individual rights and form a union with rules and regulations. Next, they would choose a leader who would enforce those rules, for better or worse. Because they had voted this ruler in place, they were stuck with him for better or worse and could not rebel against him assuming things had tilted toward the worse. After all, they voted for him!

Contra that governmental perspective is that of John Locke who, although believing some of what Hobbes did, Locke nonetheless left it up to the citizens to not only decide if the person they voted for was fulfilling his post up to their expectations but equally, if they decided he was not, they had the right to rebel against this politician's authority and overthrow him (or at least ignore him in as much as that was possible).

In other words, and as America's own founding made clear, the principle of principled rulership and the freedom to disagree and throw out an unacceptable ruler has been part and parcel of what it means to be an "American" right from the start. Indeed, this principle of keeping unwanted power at arms-length would become enshrined in our very own Constitution in the Tenth Amendment.

> ***The powers not delegated to the United States by the Constitution, nor prohibited by it to the states, are reserved to the states respectively, or to the people.***
> ***Amendment X***

It is the Tenth Amendment that can be used as the philosophical stepping-stone to decentralize. Although this Amendment is one of the original Bill of Rights it is, for the most part, long forgotten by so-called "patriots" in government service who have long forgotten this perspective of our Founding Fathers on freedom. Instead, Americans have chosen to buy into the concept of American Nationalism at the continent-wide level, and international imperialism in the drive for world government at the international level.[86]

---

[86] *Democracy: The God That Failed,* p. 112. "A decisive step in the direction of global unification was taken with the establishment of a *pax*

The Tenth Amendment was and still should be considered not as a historical anomaly from the past – but as a crucial, historical bulwark against Federal intervention into the lives of citizens at the State level. It is the Tenth Amendment that is our Constitutional guarantee against Federal usurping of power in the realm of individual citizens at the State level. It is also the Tenth Amendment that was clearly trampled on during the Civil War and throughout every decade since then as the Federal Government began to grow exponentially in its evolution into the matrix of power that it now is.

Lastly, it is the Tenth Amendment that philosophically and governmentally should be used as a rallying point when motivating

---

Americana. And indeed, throughout the entire period the U.S., Western Europe, and most of the rest of the world have suffered from a steady and dramatic growth of government power, taxation, and regulatory expropriation." See also: *Modern Times,* by Paul Johnson and *The Present Age,* by Robert Nisbet.

people to consider the possibility of peaceful secession[87] which, upon the bankruptcy of the nation and the inevitable slide toward dissolution of Federal regulation and control, will make

---

[87] In a 2004 interview, Hans-Hermann Hoppe spoke on the advantages of small independent (and wealthier) countries: "To the contrary, the greatest hope for liberty comes from the small countries: from Monaco, Andorra, Liechtenstein, even Switzerland, Hong Kong, Singapore, Bermuda, etc.; and as a liberal one should hope for a world of tens of thousands of such small independent entities. Why not a free independent city of Istanbul and Izmir, which maintain friendly relations with the central Turkish government, but which no longer make tax payments to the latter nor receive any payments from it, and which no longer recognize central government law but have their own Istanbul law or Izmir law. The apologists of the central state (and of superstates such as the EU) claim that such a proliferation of independent political units would lead to economic disintegration and impoverishment. However, not only does empirical evidence speak sharply against this claim: the above-mentioned small countries are all wealthier than their surroundings. Moreover, theoretical reflection also shows that this claim is just another statist myth." See: Venice's Secession from Italy, Hans-Hermann Hoppe, and Nation-States; March 24, 2014. www.mises.org See also: https://www.lewrockwell.com/2015/04/fred-reed/the-coming-breakup-of-the-united-states/ See also: https://www.lewrockwell.com/2015/03/lew-rockwell/get-out-peacefully/

independent republics, free states and city states a historical reality[88] as has been the case in all disintegrating empires.

The concept behind the Tenth Amendment is the idea of individual self-determination for each person as a human right contra the current perspective held by government officials who have abused it. Equally, the so-called "patriots" amongst the general populace have both forgotten and accepted the belief that individuals are nothing more than commodities for the State to use as it will.

---

[88] Ludwig von Mises, *Liberalism: In the Classical Tradition,* (Irvington-Hudson, N.Y.: Foundation for Economic Education, [1927] 1985), p.109-110. "The right of self-determination in regard to the question of membership in a state thus means: whenever the inhabitants of a particular territory, whether it be a single village, a whole district, or series of adjacent districts, make it known, by a freely conducted plebiscite, that they no longer wish to remain to a state…their wishes are to be respected and complied with. This is the only feasible and effective way of preventing revolutions and civil and international wars…If it were in any way possible to grant this right of self-determination to every individual, it would have to be done."

It is upon this "dissolution of Federal regulation and control" due to financial and political reasons that the reality of autonomous, low tax/low regulation competing entities similar to the "free states" extant in Medieval Europe will encourage people to emigrate with their talents, abilities and money to develop a life conducive to freedom, creativity and progress.[89] "Hegemonic relations are replaced by contractual, mutually beneficial, foreign relations"[90] between competing low tax areas. "To avoid the loss in particular of its most productive subjects, it [the decentralized city states or free states] comes under increased pressure to adopt comparatively liberal domestic policies by allowing more private property and imposing a lower tax and regulation burden than its neighbors. Ultimately, with as many territories as separate households,

----

[89] *Democracy: The God That Failed,* p. 110-111.
[90] *Ibid,* p. 113.

villages, or towns, the opportunity for economically motivated emigration is maximized and government power over a domestic economy minimized."[91]

"By engaging in unrestricted free trade, even the smallest territory can be fully integrated into the world market and partake of every advantage of the division of labor, and its owners may become the wealthiest people on earth."[92] "Lastly, secession promotes economic integration and development. The process of centralization has resulted in the formation of an international, U.S. − dominated government cartel of managed migration, trade, and fiat money, even more invasive and burdensome governments, globalized welfare-warfare statism and economic stagnation or even declining standards of living. Secession, if it is extensive enough, could change all of this. The world would

---

[91] *Ibid,* p. 114-115.
[92] *Ibid,* p. 115.

consist of tens of thousands of independent free cities such as the present-day "oddities" of Monaco, Andorra, San Marino, Liechtenstein, Hong Kong, and Singapore. Greatly increased opportunities for economically motivated migration would result, and the world would be one of small liberal governments economically integrated through free trade and an international commodity such as gold. It would be a world of unheard of prosperity, economic growth, and cultural advancement."[93]

In opposition to the above is of course the State. "The state – a judicial monopoly – must be recognized as the source of decivilization: states do not create law and order, they destroy it. Families and households must be recognized as the source of civilization."[94] Contra this perspective – families and households

---

[93] *Ibid,* p. 115.
[94] *Ibid,* p. 185.

being the source of civilization – and not realized by most modern conservatives is the belief that government will provide for the flourishing of civilization when ultimately, and similar to democratic or authoritarian socialism, "most contemporary conservatives (at least most of the spokesman of the conservative establishment) either do not recognize that their goal of restoring normalcy requires the most drastic, even revolutionary, anti-statist social changes, or (if they know about this) they are members of the "fifth column" engaged in destroying conservatism from inside (and hence, must be regarded as evil)"[95] as they are just as destructive of society. They lean toward the State as being the savior[96] and are actually against capitalism, free markets and trade.[97] What needs to be understood is that

---

[95] *Ibid,* p. 190.
[96] *Ibid,* p. 192.
[97] *Ibid,* p. 193.

government control, similar to socialism, always leads to the control of the people and their means of production in the name of either freeing the people from oppression or protecting them. Although the short-term goals of helping the underclass achieve a better lifestyle may seem attainable, and have small successes here and there, and for a time it appears that a populace has been made "safe for democracy" – the long-term effect of such policies is that the populace becomes oppressed, the standard of living declines, and the people remain children, sadly content to let the inefficient government do all their thinking and regulating.

It is to the family and community-focused decentralization that we must look for freedom and prosperity rather than the current form of statism that destroys them.[98] Equally, it is private ownership and

---

[98] *Ibid,* p. 197-198.

tools of production being used by the individual and families that will act as seedbeds of creativity, progress and civilization.[99] Such a society would allow the right to exclusion[100] in context of private property but that is perfectly within the right of private property owners that includes the ownership of their own tools of production.

Just as neighboring countries facilitate trade and business, so likewise would neighbors, neighborhoods and towns and cities freely be able to trade or decide not to trade[101] as they saw fit; this is what it means to be free!

> In a country, or a world, of totally private property, including streets, and of private contractual neighborhoods consisting of

---

[99] *Ibid,* p. 210-211.
[100] *Ibid,* p. 211-213.
[101] *Ibid,* p. 211-213.

property-owners, these owners can make any sort of neighborhood-contracts they wish. In practice, then, the country would be a truly "gorgeous mosaic"… ranging from rowdy Greenwich Village-type [6th street in Austin?] contractual neighborhoods, to socially conservative homogeneous WASP neighborhoods. Remember that all deeds and covenants would once again be totally legal and enforceable, with no meddling government restrictions upon them. So that considering the drug question, if a proprietary neighborhood contracted that no one would use drugs, and Jones violated the contract and used them, his fellow community-contractors would simply enforce the contract and kick him out. Or, since no advance contract can allow for all conceivable circumstances, suppose that Smith became so personally obnoxious that his fellow neighborhood-owners wanted him ejected. They would then have to buy him out - probably on terms set contractually in advance in accordance with some "obnoxious" clause.[102]

The foundation of such proprietary or covenantal communities would be based upon ownership by single proprietors, kinship relationships or a consortium of proprietors who agree in advance as to what they want to do within their community.[103]

---

[102] Murray N. Rothbard, "The 'New Fusion': A Movement For Our Time," *Rothbard-Rockwell Report* 2, no. 1 [January 1991]: 9-10.
[103] *Democracy: The God That Failed,* p. 214-215.

The Proprietor builds value in the inventory of community land chiefly by satisfying three functional requirements of a community which he alone as an owner can adequately fulfill: *selection of members, land planning,* and *leadership*... The first two functions, membership selection and land planning, are accomplished by him automatically in the course of determining to whom, and for what purpose, to let the use of land. The third function, leadership, is his natural responsibility and also his special opportunity, since his interest alone is the success of the whole community rather than that of any special interest within. Assigning land automatically established the kinds of tenants and their spatial juxtaposition to one another and, hence, the economic structure of the community...Leadership also includes arbitration of differences among tenants, as well as guidance and participation in joint efforts…[Indeed], in a fundamental sense the security of the community is a part of the owner's real estate function. Under land planning, he supervises the design of all construction from the standpoint of safety. He also chooses tenants with a view to their compatibility and complementary with other members of the community and learns to anticipate in the leases and to provide in other ways against disputes developing among tenants. By his informal peacemaking and arbitration, he resolves differences that might otherwise become serious. In these many ways he ensures "quiet possession," as it was so admirably phrased in the language of the Common Law, for his tenants.[104]

---

[104] MacCallum, *The Art of Community,* (Menlo Park, CA: Institute for Humane Studies, 1970), *p.63,66,67.*

To facilitate this would require the support of the community at large.[105] When members of this private community rebel against the covenant they would be excluded and either step back in line or have to leave.[106] Again, we are discussing the reality of a covenantal community which, similar to a homeowners association, will determine ahead of time who and what they do and do not want in their geographical area by enacting a system of private governance.[107]

Granted, in context of our modern sensibilities this proposition seems impossible, even ludicrous. But when you consider the alternative with government-run organizations, we end up with more of the same, in that decivilization occurs within communities such as small towns as well as cities. People are turned

---

[105] *Democracy: The God That Failed,* p.216.
[106] *Ibid,* p. 218.
[107] https://mises.org/library/ed-stringham-private-governance

antagonistically against one another due to political power-plays to get votes utilizing conflict between different people groups, or, as noted by Hoppe in his article *The Rise and Fall of the City,* to engender it:

> Every form of government welfare – the compulsory wealth or income transfer from "haves" to "have nots" lowers the value of a person's membership in an extended family-household system as a social system of mutual cooperation and help and assistance. Marriage loses value. For parents the value and importance of a "good" upbringing (education) of their own children is reduced. Correspondingly, for children less value will be attached, and less respect paid to their own parents. Owing to the high concentration of welfare recipients,

in the big cities family disintegration is already well advanced. In appealing to gender and generation (age) as a source of political support and promoting and enacting sex (gender) and family legislation, invariably the authority of heads of families and households and the "natural" intergenerational hierarchy within families is weakened and the value of a multigenerational family as the basic unit of human society is diminished.[108]

This reality is facilitated by politicians who are able to gain power by promising to mediate conflicts between various people groups:

---

[108] Hans-Hermann Hoppe, *The Rise and Fall of the City,* November 23, 2005.
www.mises.org/library/rise-and-fall-city

As a result of this over-proportional growth of low and even underclass people and an increasing number of ethnically, tribally, racially mixed offspring especially in the lower and lowest social strata, the character of democratic (popular) government will gradually change as well. Rather than the "race card" being essentially the only instrument of politics, politics becomes increasingly "class politics." The government rulers can and will no longer rely exclusively on their ethnic, tribal, or racial appeal and support, but increasingly they must try to find support across tribal or racial lines by appealing to the universal (not tribe or race specific) feeling of envy and egalitarianism, i.e., to social class (the untouchables or the slaves versus the masters, the workers versus the capitalists, the poor versus the rich, etc.).[109]

The increasing admixture of egalitarian class politics to the preexisting tribal policies leads to even more — racial and social — tension and hostility and to an even greater proliferation of the low and under-class population. In addition to certain ethnic or tribal groups being driven out of the cities as a result of tribal policies, increasingly also members of the upper classes of all ethnic or tribal groups will leave the city for the suburbs (only to be followed — by means of public (government) transportation — by those very people whose

---

[109] On the eliminative competition and inherent tendency of states toward centralization and territorial expansion — ultimately to the point of the establishment of a world government — see *Democracy: The God That Failed*, chapters 5, 11, and 12.

behaviors they had tried to escape).[110]

Thus, it must be understood that to avoid such a reality people must agree in advance as to what they do and do not want within their communities and plan and enact laws accordingly. The purpose of government is to enforce this local covenant. Indeed, government, similar to law, must be looked upon as the servant of the people in context of protecting their property, persons, and rights of freedom, work and ownerships rather than taxing overlords who are sources of benefits to

---

[110] See on this Helmut Schoeck, *Envy: A Theory of Social Behavior* (New York: Harcourt, Brace and World, 1970); Rothbard, *Egalitarianism as a Revolt Against Nature and Other Essays*; and esp. "Freedom, Inequality, Primitivism, and the Division of Labor," in ibid. For a sociological treatment of this second — democratic or "plebeian" — stage in the development of city government, based on and riven by classes and "class conflicts" (rather than clans and family conflicts, as during the preceding development stage of patrician government), see Max Weber, *The City*, chap. 4.

those whom they want to gather votes and political power from by means of wealth re-distribution programs and so-called "free" social services.

Classical-liberal political philosophy – as personified by Locke and most prominently displayed in Jefferson's *Declaration of Independence* – was first and foremost a moral doctrine. Drawing on the philosophy of the Stoics and the late Scholastics, it centered around the notions of self-ownership, original appropriation of nature-given (unowned) resources, property, and contract as universal human rights implied in the nature of man *qua* rational animal. In the environment of princely and royal rulers, this emphasis on the universality of human rights placed the liberal philosophy naturally in radical opposition to every established government. For a liberal, every man, whether king or peasant, was subject to the same universal and eternal principles of justice, and a government either could derive its justification from a contract between private property owners or it could not be justified at all. But could *any* government be justified?

The affirmative liberal answer is well-known. It set out from the undeniable true proposition that, mankind being what it is, murderers, robbers, thieves, thugs, and con artists will always exist, and life in society will be impossible if they are not threatened with physical punishment. In order to maintain a liberal social order, liberals insisted, it is necessary that its members be in the position to pressure (by threatening or applying violence) anyone who does not respect the life and property of others to acquiesce to the rules of society. From this correct premise, liberals concluded that this indispensable task of maintaining of law and order is the unique function of government.[111]

To facilitate such a society would require a shift from organizations with a monopoly of power to security firms that are market-oriented. Such a "shift" would ensure enforcement of only what their contract stipulates contra the current situation here in America wherein the citizens have little if any say as to what

<hr>

[111] *Ibid,* p. 225-226. See also Mises in *Liberalism: In the Classical Tradition,* p.37.

laws are enforced by police. In as much as they either do not enforce the stipulations of their agreement, or act beyond the contractual boundaries (police brutality?) of said agreement their services are terminated.[112]

Again, this flies in the face of the current socio-political structure in America – yet a simple syllogism proves the current legal/political/military situation inept in terms of meeting the needs of the average citizen. Consider the reason usually given for the necessity of the current legal system, political and military enforcement: protect the citizen against aggressors, both domestic and foreign. So far so good! Indeed, even the U.S. Constitution makes a similar statement, right? Yet we really need to ask the following questions when we consider the cost of the current services

---

[112] *Democracy: The God That Failed,* p. 225-228.

rendered by the State contra the actual results of said "services."

How can theft (via taxation) and force (applied by police if you fail to pay the government) be the solution for theft and force by criminals? How can mass warfare by the State and the subsequent loss of money, life and property be the solution to the threat of loss of life, money and property by other States? It is amazing that people do not see this reality.

In our Declaration of Independence we were told the following:

> *We hold these truths to be self-evident: that all men are created equal; that they are endowed by their Creator with inalienable rights; that among these are life, liberty, and the pursuit of happiness: that to secure these rights, governments are instituted*

*among men, deriving their just powers from the **consent of the governed***.

Yet the result has been what anyone with eyes to see can clearly see: dismal!

According to the pronouncements of our state rulers and their intellectual bodyguards (of whom there are more than ever before), we are better protected and more secure than ever. We are supposedly protected from global warming and cooling, from extinction of animals and plants, from abuses of husbands and wives, parents and employers, from poverty, disease, disaster, ignorance, prejudice, racism, sexism, homophobia, and countless other public enemies and dangers. In fact, however, matters are strikingly different. In order to provide us with all this "protection," the state managers expropriate more than 40 percent of the incomes of private producers year in and year out. Government debt and liabilities have increased uninterruptedly, thus increasing the need for future expropriations. Owing to the substitution of government paper money for gold, financial insecurity has increased sharply, and we are continually robbed through currency depreciation. Every detail of private life, property, trade, and contract is regulated by ever higher mountains of laws (legislation), thereby creating permanent legal uncertainty and moral hazard. In particular, we have been gradually stripped of the right to exclusion implied in the very concept of private property. As sellers we cannot sell to and as buyers we cannot buy from whomever we wish. And as members of associations we are not permitted to enter into whatever restrictive covenant we believe to be mutually beneficial. As Americans, we must accept immigrants we do not want as our neighbors. As teachers, we cannot get rid of ill-behaved students. As employers, we are stuck with incompetent or destructive employees. As landlords, we are forced to cope with bad tenants. As bankers and insurers, we are not allowed to avoid bad risks. As restaurant or bar owners, we must accommodate unwelcome customers. And as members of private associations, we are compelled to accept individuals and actions in violation of our own rules and restrictions. In short, the more the state has increased it expenditures on "social" security and "public" safety, the more our private property rights have been eroded, the more our property has been expropriated, confiscated, destroyed, or depreciated, and the more we have been deprived of the very foundation of all protection: economic independence, financial strength, and personal wealth. The path of every president and practically every member of Congress is littered with hundreds of thousands of nameless victims of personal economic ruin, financial bankruptcy, emergency, improvishment, despair, hardship and frustration.[113]

---

[113] *Democracy: The God That Failed,* p. 242-243.

Perhaps people should consider another part of the Declaration of Independence:

> *It is the right of the people to alter or abolish it, and to institute new government, laying its foundation on such principles, and **organizing its powers in such form, as to them shall seem most likely to affect their safety and happiness**.*

Ultimately, right wing or left wing excuses are the same.[114] All statism fails because it makes economic calculation (a.k.a. stewardship) impossible due to the hidden costs inherent within all bureaucracy wherein input/output ratios are vague, making a true cost/benefit analysis complicated.[115] So likewise the issues of defense: true costs and true benefits for

---

[114] *Ibid,* p. 244.
[115] *Ibid,* p. 245.

American wars are unknown to the average tax-paying citizen who is forced to rely on government and government-directed media for "explanations" from the "experts" all the while having the privilege of being a citizen: direct taxes via payroll or indirect via the Federal Reserve practice of inflation!

Thus, it is only through private defense firms wherein freedom of choice regarding services can take place contra collective services that cost more than the citizen wants and delivers limited "service" in the true meaning of the word.[116]

> Defense in the free society (including such defense services to person and property as police protection and judicial finds), would therefore have to be supplied by people or firms who did not – as the

---

[116] *Ibid,* p. 246-247.

State does – arrogate to themselves a compulsory monopoly of police or judicial protection...defense firms would have to be as freely competitive and as non-coercive against non-invaders as are all other suppliers of goods and services on the free market. Defense services, like all other services, would be marketable and marketable only.[117]

By utilizing defensive security firms as insurance, the price, of protection is lowered[118] because the product demanded is narrowed in context of specific requirements rather than expanded as it is with regulatory states. The purpose of government would be fixed as to what it provided its customers and that within a specific paradigm as noted by University of

---

[117] Murray N. Rothbard, *Power and Market,*
(Kansas City: Sheed Andrews and McMeel, 1997),
p. 2.
[118] *Democracy: The God That Failed,* p. 247.

Chicago law professor Richard A. Epstein in his ground breaking book, *Simple Rules for a Complex World*. He wrote the following in explanation of a simple legal concept worth building a societal legal foundation upon:

> This rule forms the basis of the law of tort. In its crudest and simplest form, the irreducible core of this body of law can be succinctly expressed: "keep off." This two-word rule accurately describes the historical and intellectual thrust of much of the common law: to prevent trespass to land, larceny, murder, rape, and (by extension) infringement of patents – and indeed interference with the exchange relationships between parties. It is amazing how much, even in this age of heightened

sensitivity to sexual harassment, you can learn about interactions between strangers by remembering to keep your hands to yourself. That precept was drummed into us as little children as one of those homespun homilies that make the world go round. But that rule also turns out to track the deep philosophical principle of respect for the autonomy of other individuals. This rule allows people to use, and use productively, the things they own without your being able to impose your will on them. And you will have the same freedom relative to them.[119]

Granted, at first blush the above quote seems simplistic, yet it acts, if nothing else,

---

[119] Richard A. Epstein, *Simple Rules for a Complex World,* (Harvard University Press: Cambridge, M.A., 1995; 1997), p. 91.

as a foundational principle by which all people (including those in government involving their relationships with the citizenry) can and should be comfortable with: prudence in human interaction. Likewise, a legal structure that the same citizens would desire to live within would allow for such principles to both flourish in society and be protected. Indeed, the whole purpose of government would be pretty much limited to such a "foundational principle" as to allow people the confidence to be able to plan for their future knowing that they did not have to continuously keep an eye and ear open for the next barrage of government interventionism.

Naturally, and as noted above, this idea too would be subject to the discretion of the local populace in a decentralized order who may in fact want such foundational principle in their city state.

Worlds and Worldviews Apart: Nuts &
Bolts

Granted, the above idea seems overwhelming at first: how would these various and competing city-states reconcile their different religious and political perspectives on law and order? What about the issues of taxation, etc? Discussions of what a society should look like are generally complicated by two factors:

1. People live within a current socio-political-economic structure that, regardless of its faults, they are comfortable with because it is "the devil that they know." People fear the unknown and this is only natural.

2. Much of our ideas, whether about politics, or anything else for that matter, are shaped by media of various types, up to and including our educational system thus we believe what we are told about our political-economic system. As noted in the

previous book titled *America's Age of Empire*, "Sadly, most people are not aware of their past, familial or national. Indeed, there is a lack of linkage to the past other than various holidays (Christmas, Thanksgiving, and July 4th) for which the true meaning has long been forgotten by the general populace. If they are historically minded, they certainly are not very motivated by it anymore as an ethos to be understood, maintained and guarded. This is why they are so easily manipulated by the ebb and flow of public opinion, the media, and government rather than guided by principle – they are not rooted."

Nonetheless, there are times in history when everything we have known as "society" and the ethos that drives it forward begins to shift for various reasons. Historically this has happened through outright war and/or major political revolutions. In other cases, particularly here in America, the shift has been more of a philosophical revolution, thus its influence took years to work out in society yet still resulted in changes. These "changes" do not seem to please anyone of any political stripe amongst the average citizen. Thus there is much discontent and disagreement as to what the solution should be (witness the impact of the Trump presidential campaign). Equally problematic is the tendency of people when confronted about the possibility of socio-political change to fall into three camps:

1. The Loyal Opposition: people who do not like what they see in American politics in general, and in Washington D.C. in specific. They would like things to return to an earlier era. When confronted with the possibility, or even *necessity* of changing the political order in America they will quickly reject the proposal. America was destined to be what it is by God (if you are

a believer of some religion) or evolution (if you are an atheist or agnostic) so then both forces, divine and historical (for lack of a better phrase) must want it that way; that's why it is what it is.

2. The Anarchists: these are people who recognize all that is wrong with America politically, similar to the Loyal Opposition, yet they insist that the best solution is complete and total dissolution not only of the United States as we now know it – but all government/political structures, period. Every man will be totally free to do whatever he wants as long as he does not hurt anyone. There will be no government or law whatsoever.

3. The World Government People: these are individuals or groups (generally liberal) who, either at a top political level, or amongst your average ordinary citizen who live in Any-town America and want the United Nations, World Bank, IMF,

World Court, etc., to run everything so that all things will be equal and we will finally have peace and prosperity (albeit, a "regulated" by the State prosperity).

All three positions are mutually exclusive as they are built upon different presuppositions about God, man, law, time and hope, Teleologically, they lead to a completely different type of lifestyle thus social structure. Equally, and of the three mentioned above, this writer believes only one and two, in the final analysis, will really drive the America of the future.

The question remains: which one will win out when the economy finally tanks? What changes amongst those three positions will allow for the principles of faith (of whatever type), family (of whatever type), and freedom that all Americans, of all walks of life, insist they want?

Consider the following inter-religious scenario: If you have a group of Christians who want to set up their own socio-political order – how would they work things out with a secular group or Muslim group? How would the inescapable points of contention between the various inter-group law forms be reconciled?

Again, the answer is simple: competing jurisdictions that are set up by, and equally insured by groups of people who have a specific world and life view that they want to live in accordance with. Rather than continue the unworkable façade of multiculturalism wherein people who do not want to live together are forced by the government to send their kids to schools they do not want or serve people or tolerate people as neighbors, customers and so forth – these competing jurisdictions of domicile would allow people to determine for themselves who they do and do not want to live and work near, as well as what legal system they do or do not want to be governed by when dealing with their own people in their own area.

Equally of note are the issues of inter-group relationships between people of contrary religious and philosophical viewpoints. Inasmuch as these people either lived in a similar geographical location or worked near one another, they would have to determine what legal system would be set up to determine in advance the rules of engagement.

Hoppe sets out the principle succinctly below:

> A system of insurers offering competing law codes would promote a tendency toward the *unification* of law. The "domestic" – Catholic, Jewish, Roman, Germanic, etc – law would apply

and be binding only on the persons and properties of the insured, the insurer, and all others insured by the same insurer under the same law. Canon law, for instance, would apply only to professed Catholics and deal solely with intra-Catholic conflict and conflict resolution. Yet it would also be possible for a Catholic to interact, come into conflict with, and wish to be protected from the subscribers of other law codes, e.g, a Muslim. From this no difficulty would arise so long as Catholic and Islamic law reached the same or a similar conclusion regarding the case and contenders at hand. But if competing law codes arrive at distinctly different conclusions (as they would in at least *some* cases by virtue of the fact that they represent *different* law codes) a problem would arise. The insured would want to be protected against the contingency of intergroup conflict, too, but "domestic" (intergroup) law would be of no avail in this regard. In fact, at a minimum two distinct "domestic" law codes would be involved, and they would come to different conclusions. In such a situation it could not be expected that one insurer and the subscribers of his law code, say that Catholics would simply subordinate their judgment to that of another insurer and his law, say that of the Muslims, or *vice versa*. Rather, each insurer – Catholic and Muslim alike – would have to contribute to the development of intergroup law, i.e., law applicable in cases of disagreement among competing insurers and law codes. And because the intergroup law provisions that an insurer offered to its clients could appear credible to them, and hence a *good*, only if and insofar as the same provisions were also accepted by other insurers (and the more of them, the better), competition would promote the development and refinement of a body of law that incorporated the widest – intergroup, cross-cultural, etc. – legal-moral consensus and agreement and thus represented the greatest common denominator among various competing law codes.[120]

Again, Richard Epstein's principles are a perfect example of what should or should not be done in Hoppe's scenario above.

---

[120] *Democracy: The God That Failed,* p. 250-251.

Inasmuch as people of differing perspectives would work or live near one another it would have to be understood in advance that there would be limits on the liability others could be held accountable for regarding intergroup conflict in certain jurisdictions. The point being – it should be the people and those agencies that they choose within a competitive, free-market system that should decides these laws and develop contractual agreements[121] rather than government bureaucrats enacting legislative, agenda based decrees.[122]

It must be remembered that the desired societal outcome is correlative to the legal code, namely, "stability and certainty rather than legislation continuously in flux."[123] In as much as people want to be able to plan for the future and feel both confident and secure in their plans, it is imperative that a

---

121 *Ibid,* p. 250.
122 *Ibid,* p. 251.
123 *Ibid,* p. 252.

legal structure be set up that provides a foundation for such confidence and security.

Equally of note, different types of risk necessitate different types of protection insurance.[124] Every location implies different risk and would be insured accordingly.[125] Hence, a stateless social defense would be both highly specific in who and what it defended, but equally limited in who and what it retaliated against.[126] By way of example is that issue of State warfare which by default involves all people in that state. States are frequently aggressive because they have a monopoly of power to force taxation on the populace to pay for military aggression. State warfare implies collateral damage because war has become total war thus time, money, resources, human life are all

---

[124] *Ibid,* p. 254-255.
[125] *Ibid,* p. 255.
[126] *Ibid,* p. 257.

focused on the destruction of the supposed enemy which, more often than not, is a government entity rather than the citizenry at large. This has resulted historically in the move from highly specific warfare to indiscriminate warfare.[127]

Contra this we have low protection costs[128] via market driven protection.[129] Whereas tax funded government agents have little incentive to perform[130] in an efficient, highly focused fashion – privately funded protection insures having every incentive to perform because they know they will lose the security contract, similar to a lawn-mowing service or car mechanic, if they did not perform the agreed upon service.[131] Equally of note, neighborhood and demographic areas would be assessed as to crime probability.[132] People would

---

[127] *Ibid, p.* 256-258.
[128] *Ibid,* 258.
[129] *Ibid,* 259.
[130] *Ibid,* 259.
[131] *Ibid,* 260.

pay only for themselves[133] as opposed to being burdened by taxes paying for issues in other cities, states, and for worldwide governmental programs up to and including endless war.

Again, and as has been suggested, it is governments that destroy neighborhoods.[134] Thus State agents are not welcome.[135] Decentralized areas cause less problems for themselves and other areas due to lack of financial capital for large scale projects, military or otherwise.[136] Governments always disarm the people[137] in their attempt to gather more and more control unto themselves. A limited security service would prevent this "temptation" from occurring due to economic reasons: the service provider has no incentive to take

---

[132] *Ibid,* 261.
[133] *Ibid,* 261.
[134] *Ibid,* 261.
[135] *Ibid,* 261.
[136] *Ibid,* 243.
[137] *Ibid,* 264.

over the neighborhood because having done so – they lose the long-term income from said area. Equally, the security service, unlike a large-scale government operation does not have the power to take over a neighborhood or city-state without becoming an outright criminal organization and the reputation to go along with it unlike governments who hide their actions under a media spread of supposed legitimacy, along with societal complacency.

The issues at hand are really quite simple, as is the proposal. It is a fallacy to think that the State exercises protective powers. It is, however, perfectly logical and normal that property owners in cooperation with others and/or market driven insurance companies are more than capable of protecting local areas. Lastly, and for the good of all, private profit and loss insurers who effectively minimize aggression (individual and state sponsored), promote peace, civilization and conflict resolution will be looked upon as the true benefactors of society rather than our current overlords who promise much yet deliver little except a tax bill.

Again, it must be stressed that private companies do not insure for risks that fall under the realm of individual responsibility (whereas the State does) only because the State used coercion to get money via taxation[138] and has money to give away. In the process, it makes those recipients dependent upon the State but equally removes, via the "free money" the resolve to stand against the State. Equally of concern is the little known fact that the Constitution contradicts the Declaration of Independence by virtue of the fact that it grants government the power to tax and legislate and enforce both all the while ignoring the Lockean/Jeffersonian promises

------

138 *Ibid,* p. 286.

for life, liberty and the pursuit of happiness
and real property.[139]

---

[139] *Ibid,* p. 279.

Conclusion

What must be returned to is the idea of separate, independent communities that live and work together for an agreed-upon goal of community development, based upon free association of citizens and the making of covenants wherein they will be governed. This concept is nothing new as America, once upon a time, was committed to light tax burdens, commodity-based money, private property, self-defense by citizenry, no standing army, free trade with others, and non-interventionism. Indeed, and as Hoppe notes for us below:

> Moreover, the American colonists demonstrated the fundamental sociological importance of the institution of covenants: of associations of linguistically, ethnically, religiously, and

culturally homogeneous settlers led by and subject to the internal jurisdiction of a popular leader-founder to ensure peaceful human cooperation and maintain law and order.[140]

The reality of what Hoppe calls for here in America is, in spite of what people think, nothing new. Indeed, the French writer Alexis de Tocqueville noted the following in his book *Democracy in America*:

---

[140] *Ibid,* p. 268. Hoppe also notes: "the settlement of the North American continent confirmed the elementary sociological insight that all human societies are the outgrowth of families and kinship systems and hence, are characterized by a high degree of internal homogeneity, i.e., that "likes" typically associate with "likes" and distance and separate themselves from "unlikes." Thus, for instance, in accordance with this general tendency, Puritans preferably settled in New England, Dutch Calvinists in New York, Quakers in Pennsylvania and the southern parts of New Jersey, Catholics in Maryland, and Anglicans as well as French Huguenots in the Southern colonies." See further on this David Hackett Fisher, *Albion's Seed: Four British Folkways in America* (New York: Oxford University Press, 1989).

Here it is a question only of the associations that are formed in civil life and which have an object that is in no way political. The political associations that exist in the United States form only a detail in the midst of the immense picture that the sum of associations presents there.

Americans of all ages, all conditions, all minds constantly unite. Not only do they have commercial and industrial associations in which all take part, but they also have a thousand other kinds: religious, moral, grave, futile, very general and very particular, immense and very small; Americans use associations to give fêtes, to found seminaries, to build inns, to raise churches, to distribute books, to send missionaries to the antipodes; in this manner they create hospitals, prisons, schools. Finally, if it is a question of bringing to light a truth or developing a sentiment with the support of a great example, they associate. Everywhere that, at the head of a new undertaking, you see the government in France and a great lord in England, count on it that you will perceive an association in the United States.

In America I encountered sorts of associations of which, I confess, I had no idea, and I often admired the infinite art with which the inhabitants of the United States managed to fix a common goal to the efforts of many men and to get them to advance to it freely.

I have since traveled through England, from which the Americans took some of their laws and many of their usages, and it appeared to me that there they were very far from making as constant and as skilled a use of association.[141]

With the bankruptcy of the State will come the rise of free territories. Whether by charters granted by the collapsing government,[142] thus allowing for the Charter Colonies noted earlier, or nullification of Federal Laws and control at the State level up to an including outright secession[143] – freedom will come, and with

---

[141] http://www.press.uchicago.edu/Misc/Chicago/80532 8.html

[142] *Democracy: The God That Failed,* p. 287.

[143] https://www.lewrockwell.com/2015/04/fred-

it private property and efficiency of justice via private security insurance organizations contra State monopoly.[144] Then will come the protective services people want and will be freely willing and able to deal with and pay for as they will have freely chosen it. Equally will come the use that Americans make of association in civil life, as Tocqueville noted above, wherein people freely associate to accomplish goals to make their lives, and the lives of others around them better and all without the help of large, mega-state governments. Such a society will be a natural ordering of people, places and things as opposed to an artificial order imposed by the State.[145]

It is out of such communities[146] that the Natural Order of both society and human

---

reed/the-coming-breakup-of-the-united-states/
[144] *Democracy: The God That Failed,* p. 283.
[145] http://www.thedailybell.com/news-analysis/warning-government-is-in-danger-of-going-extinct/
[146] See Appendix on: Free Private Cities: The Future of Governance is Private as an example.

leadership as noted in an earlier chapter shall arise due to the choice of the local people.[147]

---

[147] Exodus 18:17-26.

Free Private Cities: The Future of Governance is Private

By Titus Gebel

Imagine a private company offers you the basic services of a state, i.e. protection of life, liberty and property in a defined territory. You pay a certain amount for those services per year. Your respective rights and duties are laid down in a written agreement between you and the provider. For everything else, you do what you want. Thus, you are a contracting party on an equal footing with a secured legal position, instead of subject to the government's or majority's ever changing will. And you only become a part of it if you like the offer.

Let us analyze the market for governance: states exist, at least in part, because there is demand for them. A functioning state offers a stable framework of law and order, which enables the coexistence and interaction of a large number of people. This is so attractive that most people are willing to accept significant limitations on their personal freedom in exchange. Probably even most North Koreans would prefer staying in their country, compared to living free but alone as a Robinson Crusoe on a remote island. Humans are social animals.

However, if you could offer the services of a state and also avoid its disadvantages, you would have created a better product. But after decades of political activity, I have come to the conclusion that real liberty, in the sense of voluntariness and self-determination, can't be achieved by tinkering with existing states through the democratic process. There is simply not enough demand for these values.

However, someone could offer this as a niche product for interested parties. It might be possible for private companies to provide all of the necessary services that government normally monopolizes. I have started such a company: Free Private Cities Ltd (freeprivatecities.com).

The market of living together

All that we know from the free market could be applied to what I call the "market of living together": voluntary exchange (including the right to reject any offer), competition between products, and the resulting diversity of the product range. A "state service provider" or "government services provider" could offer a specific model of living together within a defined territory and only the ones who like the offer settle there. Such offers have to be attractive — otherwise there will be no customers.

And this is exactly the idea of a *Free Private City*: a voluntary, for-profit, private enterprise that offers protection for life, liberty, and property in a given territory — better, cheaper, and freer than existing state models. Residence would depend on a predefined contractual relationship between residents and the operator.

A *FreePrivate City* as I propose it is based on the following principles:

1) Every resident has the right to live an independent life without the interference of others.

2) The interaction between the residents happens on a voluntary basis, not based on coercion. Participating and remaining in the *Free Private City* is strictly voluntary.

3) The respective rights of others must be honored, even if one does not like their way of life or attitude.

4) There is complete freedom of speech with one exception: If you are promoting expropriation or violence against others, you have to leave. The pure criticism of other people, ideologies, religions, etc. has to be accepted. "Feeling outraged" justifies no limitation of free speech.

5) The operator of the *Free Private City* ensures a stable regulatory framework and a basic infrastructure. This includes the establishment of a police, fire-fighters, emergency rescue and furthermore, the establishment of a legal framework and independent courts, so that property ownership is registered bindingly and

residents can assert their legitimate claims in a regulated process, if they are unable to agree on arbitration.

6) The framework is laid down between the residents and the operator in a contract which holds all the respective rights and obligations. This includes the consideration for every inhabitant for the operator's services. Every resident has a legal claim that his contract is performed and can claim damages for nonperformance. This contract is basically one's personal "constitution" which is superior to all existing constitutions since it may not be changed unilaterally later, neither by the operator nor by majority vote.

7) All adult residents are responsible for the consequences of their actions, not "society" or the operator. Again, there is no "human right" to live at the expense of others.

8) Conflicts of interest between residents or between residents and the operator are negotiated by independent courts or arbitral tribunals. Their decisions must be respected. Namely conflicts with the operator, e.g.

about interpretation of the contract, go to arbitration, not to courts of the operator.

9) There is no legal entitlement to join the *Free Private City*. The operator can reject candidates at his discretion. People who openly declare views that are not compatible with a free society, e.g. socialists, fascists or islamists, or known criminals, won't get admittance.

10) Each resident may terminate the contract at any time and leave the city again, but the operator may –after a trial period- cancel only for cause, as for breach of the basic rules.

Free Private Cities are not meant as a retreat for the rich. Run properly, they would develop along the lines of Hong Kong, offering opportunities to rich and poor alike. New residents who are willing to work but without means could negotiate a deferral of their payment obligations, and employers seeking a workforce could take over their contractual payment obligations.

The incentive for the operator of a *Free Private City* would be profit: offering an attractive product at the right price. This would include some public goods as mentioned as well as some infrastructure, clean environment and a set of social rules. But the operator's main service is to ensure that the free order is not disturbed and that residents' life and property are secure.

In practice, the operator can only guarantee this if he can control who is coming (prevention) and is entitled to throw out disrupters (reaction). For everything beyond this framework, there are private entrepreneurs, insurance, and civil society groups. Of course, all activity ends where the rights of others are infringed. Other than that, the proper corrective is competition and demand.

Competition and Exit

Will the threat of competition bring sufficient protection to the residents? Consider this: the Principality of Monaco is a constitutional monarchy. It concedes *zero* political participation rights for residents without Monegasque citizenship — some 80 percent of the population, including myself. Nevertheless, there are far more applicants for residency than the small housing market of this tiny place (two square kilometers) may take. Why is this so? Three reasons: there are no direct taxes in Monaco for individuals; it is extremely secure; and the government leaves you alone. If Monaco changed this, people would just move away to other jurisdictions. Thus, despite the prince's formal position of great power, competition with other jurisdictions — not separation of powers, not a constitution, and not voting — ensures the residents' freedom.

Similar in *Free Private Cities*: if the government provider sticks to his few core areas, there is no need for political participation. The idea is to have the greatest possible self-determination, not to ensure maximum participation. Accordingly, there is also no need for parliaments. Rather, such representative bodies are a constant danger to liberty, since special interest groups inevitably hijack and mutate them into self-service stores for the political class.

Competition has been proven as the only effective method in human history for limitation of power. In a *Free Private City*, contract and arbitration are efficient tools in favor of the residents. But ultimately, it is competition and the possibility of a speedy exit that guarantee that the operator remains a service provider and does not become a dictator.

A *Free Private City* is not a utopian, constructivist idea. Instead, it is simply a business model whose elements are already known and which are merely transferred to another sector, namely the market of living together. In essence, the operator is a mere service provider establishing and maintaining the framework within which the society can develop, with open outcome. The only permanent requirement in favor of freedom and self-determination is the contract with the operator. Only this contract creates mandatory obligations. For example, residents can agree on establishing a council. But even if 99% of the residents support the idea and voluntarily submit to the council's decisions, this body has no right to impose his ideas on the remaining 1%. Think of ideas like financing a public swimming pool, a social security system or establishing a minimum wage. And this is the crucial point, which failed regularly in past and present systems: the permanent guarantee of individual liberty.

How to start

In order to initiate this project, autonomy from existing sovereignties must be secured. It need not entail complete territorial independence, but it must include the right to regulate the city's internal affairs. The establishment of a Free Private City therefore requires first an agreement with an existing state. The parent state grants the operator the right to establish a *Free Private City* and to set its own rules within a defined territory, ideally with access to the sea and formerly uninhabited.

Existing states can be sold on this concept when they can expect to reap benefits from it. The quasi-city states of Hong Kong, Singapore, and Monaco have a cordon of densely populated and affluent areas adjacent to their borders. These areas are part of the parent states and their residents pay taxes to the mother country. Now, if such structures are formed around a previously underdeveloped or unpopulated area, this is a gain for the parent state. Negotiating with a government to surrender partial sovereignty is certainly no easy task, but it is in my view more promising than attempts to "change the system from within."

Free Private Cities are much more than just a nice idea for a few people on the margins. They have the potential to subject existing states to creative destruction. If *Free Private Cities* are developed across the world, they will put states under considerable pressure to change their systems towards more freedom, or else they may lose subjects and revenue. And this is precisely this positive effect of competition that has been lacking in the state market to date. Not all *Free Private Cities* need conform to my own ideal rules. Specialized cities offering social security or catering to specific religious, ethnical or ideological concerns are conceivable. Within this framework, even socialists would be free to try to prove that their system *done properly* really does work. But this time one thing is different: others do not have to suffer from this (or any other) social experiment. The superstructure of voluntary association allows many different systems to flourish. Given voluntary participation, everything is possible.

This simple rule has the potential to disarm and transform even a totalitarian ideology into just one product among many. I firmly believe that *Free Private Cities* or similar autonomous regions are inevitable. People of all social and economic groups will not forever agree to be looted, bullied, and patronized by the political class, without ever having a meaningful choice. *Free Private Cities* are a peaceful, voluntary alternative that can transform our societies without revolution or violence — or even majority consensus. My guess: we will see the first *Free Private City* within the next ten years. I hope to see you there.

https://www.startupsocieties.com/post/free-private-cities-the-future-of-governance-is-private

Titus Gebel is a German entrepreneur with a PhD in law. He founded amongst others Deutsche Rohstoff AG (__WWW.ROHSTOFF.DE__) and now lives with his family in Monaco. After 30 years of political activity he came to the conclusion that freedom cannot be achieved in the democratic process. His solution: create an entirely new product that will work as a role model in case of success. He is currently working on a book about Free Private Cities and will subsequently put the idea into practice.

www.ingramcontent.com/pod-product-compliance
Lightning Source LLC
Chambersburg PA
CBHW061340250726
48657CB00004B/1260